BACKROAD WINERIES OF CALIFORNIA

Bill Gleeson

CHRONICLE BOOKS
San Francisco

Printed in the United States of America.

LIBRARY OF CONGRESS CATALOGING IN PUBLICATION DATA

Gleeson, Bill.
    Backroad wineries of California.

    Includes index.
    1. Wine and wine-making—California. I. Title.
TP557.G57 1985   641.2′2′09794   84-28520
ISBN 0-87701-318-7

Editing: Deborah Stone
Cover Illustration: Beth Whybrow Leeds
Book and cover design: Thomas Ingalls + Associates
Composition: On Line Typography

Chronicle Books
One Hallidie Plaza
San Francisco, CA 94102

CONTENTS

Introduction

If mention of a trip to the wine country conjures up visions of Napa Valley giants such as Sterling, Beaulieu, Mondavi, and Inglenook, you're by no means alone. During peak tourist days, an estimated 14,000 cars and buses make their way—slowly—along Highway 29 between Napa and Calistoga. Some claim this region to be second only to Disneyland as California's biggest tourist draw.

Consequently, if you're expecting quiet tasting rooms and a peaceful drive along the scenic highway, you'll no doubt be surprised to encounter bumper-to-bumper traffic on the road and elbow-to-elbow traffic in the tasting rooms.

That is, of course, unless you forsake the crowded highways for the backroads of Northern California's hidden wine country. While out-of-the-way wineries actually outnumber those adjacent to California's thoroughfares, attention is often focused on the more easily accessible establishments.

So, instead of competing with bus and tourist traffic along State Route 29, why not explore the hills on either side of Napa Valley? For example, enchanting Mayacamas Winery above St. Helena has a narrow, bumpy driveway no tour bus driver would dare attempt. And, while guides will whisk you and a few hundred others through some of the valley's large, state-of-the-art production facilities, David Clark will personally show you around his century-old, stone-walled Deer Park Winery, just a few miles off the Silverado Trail.

Similar alternatives exist in other wine-growing regions of the north state. Those who venture up to the Uvas Valley from Gilroy or Watsonville have an opportunity to enjoy an unhurried visit with amiable Nikola Kirigin-Chargin, who not only makes the wine for Kirigin Cellars but pours it for visitors.

If your wine country visits have been confined to the major highways, chances are the establishments listed in the following pages are unfamiliar. In terms of production, they vary considerably—from a couple of thousand to more than 50,000 cases per year. There are other similarities, however. The owners tend to play personal if not exclusive roles in the production of their product; all extend a friendly welcome to visitors—though some require a phone call in advance; and each is pleasantly situated off the beaten path in rural areas of Northern and Central California.

This isn't to say that trips to the major wine-producing establishments should be discouraged. On the contrary, their modern equipment and techniques are impressive examples of winemaking technology and are well worth a visit, especially by first-time winery sojourners.

But there is another overlooked world out there. Few wine experiences can rival a visit with—or tour or tasting led by— a vintner who, at many backroad wineries, is responsible for tending the vines, operating the crusher, and polishing the bottles.

Finally, don't let a "by appointment" notice discourage you. Such requests are by no means designed to dissuade visits. Because many small wineries are mom- and pop-type operations, guests who drop in without notice might find the proprietors out in the fields, working in the cellar, or otherwise occupied. For most, a phone call twenty-four hours in advance of a visit is sufficient. The call will be appreciated by the winemaker— and is well worth the effort to the visitor.

THE SONOMA AND MENDOCINO COUNTY REGION

This Is Where it all Began

In the categories of natural beauty, history, and diversity of wineries, the Sonoma and Mendocino County areas are unsurpassed. From the lush redwood forests of the Russian River Valley to the rolling hills east of Ukiah, the scenery is nothing short of spectacular. Recreational opportunities abound here.

The area's history is intricately tied to the grape. Agoston Haraszthy was the first to tap the commercial grape-growing potential of the Sonoma Valley—and of California, for that matter. Known as the father of California winemaking, Haraszthy established Buena Vista Winery—the state's first—and cultivated what once was the largest vineyard in the world. Your backroad tour of the Sonoma and Mendocino wine country begins, appropriately enough, at Haraszthy's old cellars.

Those who followed the pioneer over the years have brought with them unique touches that set this region apart from all others. Even within an appellation (and there are many here), the individuality of different winemakers shines for all to enjoy. In the warm Alexander Valley near Healdsburg, for example, Alexander Valley Vineyards is headquartered in a contemporary, Spanish-style structure consisting of an adobe cellar topped with a veranda-shaded, board and batten tasting room. Just down the road Field Stone Winery sits below a grassy knoll, a natural stone facade providing the only clue to its subterranean existence.

Several other distinctive wineries call this region home. Hop Kiln Winery is housed in an architecturally significant hop kiln, while Hacienda Wine Cellars utilizes an old hospital. Farther north near Ukiah, the owners of McDowell Valley Vineyards constructed a modern solar facility to showcase their wares.

Some forty wineries between Santa Rosa and Cloverdale are listed in a guide published by the Russian River Wine Road. Should your visit include an overnight stay, you'll also be interested in the guide's listing of resorts, motels, and bed and breakfast inns. For details, consult the Grape Escapes section at the back of this book.

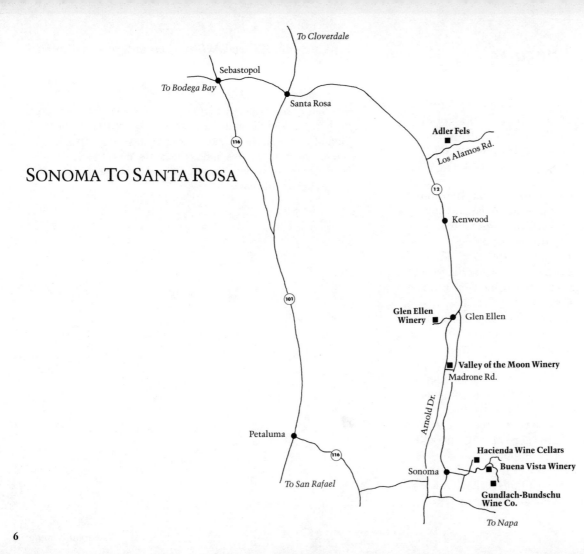

SONOMA TO SANTA ROSA

To Cloverdale

Sebastopol

To Bodega Bay

Santa Rosa

116

Adler Fels

Los Alamos Rd.

12

Kenwood

Glen Ellen Winery

Glen Ellen

101

Valley of the Moon Winery

Madrone Rd.

Arnold Dr.

Petaluma

116

Hacienda Wine Cellars

Buena Vista Winery

Sonoma

Gundlach-Bundschu Wine Co.

To San Rafael

To Napa

Buena Vista Winery and Vineyards

Sonoma

For those with even the slightest interest in California wine, a visit to Buena Vista Winery on the outskirts of Sonoma is a must. It was here that the state's wine industry began more than 100 years ago.

If Buena Vista is the birthplace of California wines, Agoston Haraszthy, the Hungarian aristocrat turned California vintner, must be the patriarch of the industry.

A one-time bodyguard of Emperor Ferdinand of Austria-Hungary, Haraszthy fled his homeland after being marked for death following a revolution in the 1840s. He landed in the United States and traveled from east to west scouting a vineyard site. Haraszthy's twelve-year search ended in the Sonoma Valley, where he built a winery in 1857.

Tunnels were carved into a hill of solid limestone; rock debris was shaped into blocks for construction of the exterior walls. (While the sturdy winery has survived for more than a century, the wine pioneer's palatial home was destroyed by a fire before 1900.)

In 1861 Haraszthy convinced the governor of California to send him to Europe to collect vinifera vines. "The Count" returned with some 100,000 cuttings which were distributed to growers throughout the region. In the years immediately following Haraszthy's death in 1869, the vineyard at Buena Vista was the largest in the world, boasting nearly a half-million cuttings.

Haraszthy's wine empire wasn't spared, however, from a devastating *phylloxera* plague nor from the 1906 earthquake during which the Buena Vista tunnels collapsed. The operation bounced back in 1943 when the vineyards were replanted and buildings were restored by Frank Bartholomew.

Tastings take place today in the original press house, a fine stone building with tile floors and an art gallery on the second level. Visitors may guide

18000 Old Winery Road
Sonoma, CA 95476
(707) 938-1266

HOURS: 10 A.M.–5 P.M. daily
TASTINGS: Yes
TOURS: Yes, self-guided
PICNIC AREA: Yes
RETAIL SALES: Yes
DIRECTIONS: From downtown Sonoma, east on East Napa Street, left on Old Winery Road to winery gate.
VINTNER'S CHOICE: Gewurztraminer

themselves through the old cellar where historical information and photos tell the Haraszthy story. This facility serves as headquarters for the Knights of the Vine, the nation's only wine brotherhood.

Unbeknownst to most who visit the historic Sonoma winery, there is another large, state-of-the-art facility operated by Buena Vista in the Carneros district. The new winery is equipped to crush 150 tons of grapes per day and has a storage capacity of nearly one million gallons.

Fortunately, the German corporation that owns Buena Vista has imposed no such modern trappings on Haraszthy's old stomping grounds in Sonoma. In fact, vehicular traffic here has wisely been restricted from the winery area, which further enhances the vintage ambience at this California wine shrine.

Hacienda Wine Cellars

Sonoma

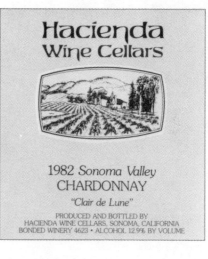

Hacienda Wine Cellars shares with its neighbor, Buena Vista Winery, the historic vineyard cultivated by California wine pioneer Agoston Haraszthy in the mid-nineteenth century.

The vast plantings, which at one time had no equal in the world, were rescued from years of neglect in 1941 by Frank Bartholomew, former head of United Press International. Over the next several years, Bartholomew pumped new life into Haraszthy's historic Buena Vista Winery and replanted the vineyards. He sold Buena Vista sometime later, retaining only fifty acres of vines.

His absence from the winemaking scene was shortlived, however. The lure of the grape brought Bartholomew back into the business in 1973 when he transformed the old Sonoma Valley Hospital into Hacienda Wine Cellars. A. Crawford Cooley, a successful businessman whose family has owned vineyard land in Sonoma County for more than a century, is now the primary stockholder and president of Hacienda.

The 1920s-era Mediterranean-style building, whose original purpose was the care of patients, turned out to be equally well suited to the care of wine. Fourteen-inch-thick brick walls help maintain a fairly consistent temperature for the aging vintages. The production area is sealed off from the tasting room by a glass door through which visitors can catch a glimpse of fancy chandeliers that illuminate rows of neatly stacked barrels along a tiled floor.

Outside, a row of ornamental vines shares the front yard with a number of plants and trees. The well-manicured gardens here are a favorite of picnickers who congregate at tables under spreading oak trees.

1000 Vineyard Lane
Sonoma, CA 95476
(707) 938-3220

HOURS: 10 A.M.–5 P.M. daily
TASTINGS: Yes
TOURS: By appointment
PICNIC AREA: Yes
RETAIL SALES: Yes
DIRECTIONS: From downtown Sonoma, east on East Napa Street, left on East Seventh Street; follow signs to Vineyard Lane.
VINTNER'S CHOICE: Gewurztraminer and Chardonnay

Gundlach-Bundschu Wine Company

Vineburg

Jacob Gundlach's persistent struggle to start a new life as a California winemaker was marked both by hardship and good fortune. First there was the storm that wrecked his ship on the trip around Cape Horn from Europe. He spent forty-nine days as an island castaway before reaching San Francisco in 1851.

Next came the backbreaking cultivation of his 400-acre Rhinefarm in Sonoma Valley with a horse-drawn single blade plow, and the arduous process of hand-picking grapes and hauling sixty-pound lugs.

In 1874 the destructive insect called *Phylloxera* worked its way through California's vineyards and into Gundlach's prized vines. Fortunately, Rhinefarm vineyard master Julius Dresel discovered that native American vines resisted the disease, and work began to graft the domestic rootstock onto the existing vines.

Things improved over the next few years as Jacob and his partner, son-in-law Charles Bundschu, built a thriving business, winning a loyal following and prestigious awards for their wines.

Tragedy struck again in 1906 when Jacob watched the great earthquake and fire turn his San Francisco cellars into ashes. Rhinefarm was untouched, however, and the business continued.

The next disastrous blow was dealt not by nature but by the government. Although the vineyards were cultivated during Prohibition, the winery closed its doors and Gundlach-Bundschu was disbanded. A fire later gutted the abandoned winery.

Walter Bundschu, Jacob's great-grandson, took over the operation and was succeeded by his son, Towle Bundschu. Towle's son Jim revitalized the company by rebuilding the winery in the early 1970s using stone from the original building. The production area occupies most of the building. The tasting area is inside the front door, over which hangs an old bell from the original vineyards. Jacob Gundlach would have been proud.

3775 Thornsberry Road
Vineburg, CA 95487
(707) 938-5277

HOURS: 11 A.M.–4:30 P.M.
TASTINGS: Yes
TOURS: No
PICNIC AREA: Yes
RETAIL SALES: Yes
DIRECTIONS: From Sonoma, east on Napa Street, left on Old Winery Road, right on Lovall Valley Road, right on Thornsberry to winery gate.
VINTNER'S CHOICE: Merlot

Valley of the Moon Winery

Glen Ellen

Harry Parducci has spent much of his life at Valley of the Moon Winery. His father, Enrico, bought the business in 1941, acquiring an assortment of buildings along with vineyards that dated back to 1851.

The younger Parducci worked with his father for a number of years before assuming the helm in 1971. Harry's sons have more recently joined the family business.

Valley of the Moon produces some 48,000 cases each year from its facilities near Sonoma Creek. Wine buffs are unfortunately limited to the harvest period for a view of the inner workings. During most of the year, visits are confined to a small tasting room at the front of the winery, under the spreading branches of a formidable bay laurel.

Valley of the Moon rounds out its roster of estate-bottled, 100 percent varietal and table wines with a selection of dessert wines, as well as champagne.

777 Madrone Road
Glen Ellen, CA 95442
(707) 996-6941

HOURS: 10 A.M.–5 P.M. Friday–Wednesday
TASTINGS: Yes
TOURS: During harvest
PICNIC AREA: Yes
RETAIL SALES: Yes
DIRECTIONS: Four miles west of Highway 12 on Madrone Road near Arnold Drive.
VINTNER'S CHOICE: White Zinfandel

Glen Ellen Winery

Glen Ellen

Upon discovering a derelict vineyard in 1979 on writer Jack London's old stomping grounds, Mike Benziger placed an excited call to his parents home in White Plains, New York. "Dad, I've found it!" he told Bruno Benziger, signaling the beginning of a new life for the family and the birth of Glen Ellen Winery.

Several years earlier, Mike had moved to California to learn the art of winemaking and to find a spot where his family could make wine together. After Mike's discovery, brothers Joe and Jerry and their families; younger brother Chris; sister Kathy; Bruno and Helen Benziger; and Bruno's mother, Katherine—thirteen in all—packed up and left their native New York, settling into two old homes on the property in the hills above Glen Ellen.

The neglected vineyards had seen many a harvest since the late 1860s when Julius Wegener was given 122 acres by Mexican Gov. Mariano Vallejo. In addition to a winemaking operation, Wegener's ranch served as a popular resort. The two residences built by Wegener today house the Benziger clan. A building that doubled in the old days as a church and dance hall stood where the swimming pool is now.

Although Wegener's family lived on the ranch for many years after his death, the vineyards declined. Nevertheless, some wine was marketed: An old Wegener diary contains references to purchases by Jack London, whose ranch was next door.

In restoring the tired estate, the Benzigers revived the two houses using period materials and furnishings. Most of the vines were replanted. A classic wooden barn is used for winemaking. A tasting area shares the building with barrels and fermenting tanks.

Visitors who have questions about the making of Glen Ellen wines need only ask the nearest person. Odds are he or she will be a Benziger.

1883 London Ranch Road
Glen Ellen, CA 95442
(707) 996-1066

HOURS: 10 A.M.–4 P.M. daily
TASTINGS: Yes
TOURS: Yes
PICNIC AREA: Yes
RETAIL SALES: Yes
DIRECTIONS: From Arnold Road in Glen Ellen, 1 mile up London Ranch Road to winery gate.
VINTNER'S CHOICE: Sauvignon Blanc

Adler Fels

Santa Rosa

Of the wineries I have visited, none appears so much a product of a single individual as Adler Fels. This is, quite literally, the winery that David Coleman built.

A graphic designer by original trade, David was introduced to the wine industry in 1974 while conceiving the label design for Chateau St. Jean. One assignment led to another, and before long David had earned a reputation as one of California's premier wine label designers. In the process he also learned a great deal about the art of winemaking.

David's decision to start a winery was hatched in 1979 during an evening of intemperate wine tasting with friend and current partner Pat Heck. Ground was broken in 1979 on a tree-studded hilltop overlooking much of Sonoma Valley. David constructed the winery by hand, adding a tower and cupola that give the building a fairytale appearance from the approaching drive.

The interior, absent any such flourishes, is intended for serious winemaking. Here stands a row of special fermentors designed by the owner. It was David who perfected the variable-capacity fermentation tank whose free-floating top adjusts to the level of wine inside. Such tanks are now in use throughout the state.

David's influence doesn't stop here, for after the aging process, the wines are bottled under a label designed by—guess who?

Adler Fels (German for "Eagle Rock," the name of a landmark outcropping visible from the winery tower) does rely also on the talents of others, including Ayn Ryan and partner, Pat. Ayn (pronounced Ann) joined the business in 1980 to direct sales efforts and shortly thereafter married David. Reminiscing about the frantic pace of Adler Fels' initial year, Ayn recalled that, "After surviving our first crush, we figured together we could make anything work." They're off to a promising start.

5325 Corrick Lane
Santa Rosa, CA 95405
(707) 539-3123

HOURS: By appointment
TASTINGS: By appointment
TOURS: By appointment
PICNIC AREA: No
RETAIL SALES: Yes, by appointment
DIRECTIONS: From Highway 12, 2 miles north on Los Alamos Road to Corrick Lane and winery gate.
VINTNER'S CHOICE: Fume Blanc

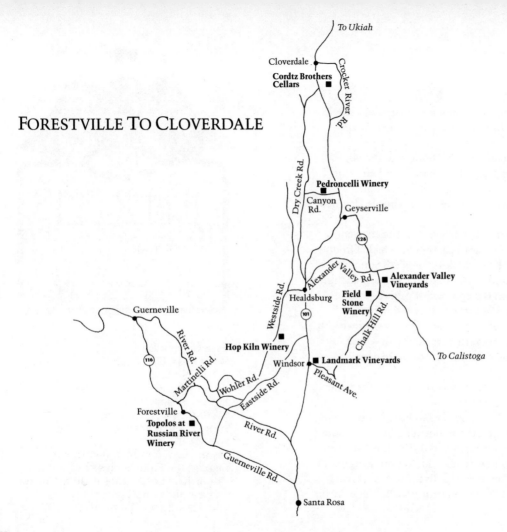

FORESTVILLE TO CLOVERDALE

To Ukiah

Cloverdale

Cordtz Brothers Cellars ■

Crocker River Rd.

Dry Creek Rd.

Pedroncelli Winery ■

Canyon Rd.

Geyserville

128

Alexander Valley Rd.

Alexander Valley Vineyards ■

Westside Rd.

Healdsburg

Field Stone Winery ■

101

Chalk Hill Rd.

To Calistoga

Guerneville

River Rd.

Martinelli Rd.

116

Hop Kiln Winery ■

Windsor

Landmark Vineyards ●

Wohler Rd.

Eastside Rd.

Pleasant Ave.

Forestville

Topolos at Russian River Winery ■

River Rd.

Guerneville Rd.

Santa Rosa ●

Topolos at Russian River Vineyards

Forestville

Question: What do you get by crossing the architecture of a hop kiln with that of Fort Ross? Answer: A decidedly unique winery.

The concrete and redwood building that now houses Topolos at Russian River Winery is a peculiar hybrid. Its builders combined striking elements of the region's old hop kilns with nineteenth century Russian architecture found at the coastal settlement of Fort Ross. The weathered building has undoubtedly sparked the curiosity of many who travel the Gravenstein Highway between Guerneville and Sebastopol.

The winery was founded in 1978 by vintner Michael Topolos and his brother, Jerry, a Bay Area businessman. Michael was motivated by years of touring European wineries as a "merchant du vin" for a San Francisco grocer and by studies at University of California, Davis. He is also an author of California wine books and has taught wine appreciation courses at area colleges.

The unusual looking winery is only part of the Russian River Vineyards complex. The establishment is one of few in California with a full restaurant. The quaint dining room is housed on the upper level of an adjacent century-old residence. The bottom portion serves as a tasting room. Among the wines available here is a Gravenstein Blanc, made from locally grown apples.

5700 Gravenstein Highway
Forestville, CA 95436
(707) 887-2956

HOURS: 10:30 A.M.–5 P.M. Wednesday–
    Sunday
TASTINGS: Yes
TOURS: By appointment
PICNIC AREA: No
RETAIL SALES: Yes
DIRECTIONS: In Forestville on Highway
    116.
VINTNER'S CHOICE: Gravenstein Blanc

26 *Hop Kiln*

Hop Kiln Winery

Healdsburg

Question Martin Griffin about his seemingly peculiar combination of careers in public health and winemaking and he'll remind you of Louis Pasteur, noted bacteriologist and chief winemaker for France. The Griffin name isn't likely to go down in history with that of Pasteur, but Martin's contributions to both fields have earned him great respect throughout Northern California.

His first career included nearly twenty years as a doctor of internal medicine at a Marin County clinic he helped establish. Martin later switched careers for a brief time, performing wildlife work in such locales as Hawaii and India. He subsequently earned a master's degree in public health and became a public health officer at Sonoma State Hospital.

While he had since the 1960s held the ingredients for a winemaking operation (a 240-acre Healdsburg ranch with several acres of vines), it wasn't until the 1970s that Martin turned serious attention to establishing a winery.

The logical site was a turn-of-the-century hop kiln and cooling and baling barn which he and friends painstakingly restored from a crumbling hulk. Martin chose as his residence a stately Italianate Victorian which was moved in pieces from Fulton and reassembled next to the kiln. The establishment opened as Hop Kiln Winery in 1975.

Visitors are received in the spacious barn-turned-tasting room behind the tall kilns. A row of picture windows along the back wall illuminates a rustic interior and reveals the sweeping vista of vineyards and adjacent pond. Picnic tables are set up along the edge of the water.

While Hop Kiln has won numerous wine awards, Martin is most proud of the preservation efforts that pumped new life into the old barn and kiln. His pride is shared by the federal government, which has confirmed the winery's place in the future by declaring Hop Kiln a National Trust.

Russian River Valley
1981 Zinfandel
Alcohol 13.3% by Volume

Produced and Bottled by the Hop Kiln Winery at Griffin Vineyard, Healdsburg, Sonoma County, California

6050 Westside Road
Healdsburg, CA 95448
(707) 433-6491

HOURS: 10 A.M.–5 P.M. daily
TASTINGS: Yes
TOURS: By appointment
PICNIC AREA: Yes
RETAIL SALES: Yes
DIRECTIONS: From Mill Street in Healdsburg, south on Westside Road to winery.
VINTNER'S CHOICE: Zinfandel

Landmark Vineyards

Windsor

Notwithstanding the creep of development around the Sonoma County town of Windsor, Landmark Vineyards has managed to maintain its bucolic setting amid century-old stands of trees and acres of vineland.

A winery only since 1974, the "home ranch," as the owners refer to it, originally was a portion of a land grant that was settled in 1849 by the McClellan family. A stately Spanish-style residence was built several years later by a McClellan heir and later was home to the shipping magnate, William Matson-Roth.

The house now holds the tasting room and offices of Landmark Vineyards, established by William Mabry, Jr.; his wife, Maxine; and son, William III. Young Bill is winemaker and president of Landmark.

The purchase of the Windsor estate was the Mabrys' third and final step toward establishing their winemaking operation. The family had in the preceding two years bought grape-growing land in Sonoma and Alexander Valleys.

On the historic home ranch the Mabrys built a modern winery that draws its design inspiration from the adjacent main house. Since its first crush, Landmark has limited its production to just three wines: Cabernet Sauvignon, Chardonnay, and a proprietary white called Petit Blanc.

Visitors enter the property via an avenue flanked by towering cypress trees planted by the ranch founders. Equally impressive are the gardens, also dating from long ago. A wooded creekside area, open to Landmark guests, holds picnic tables and an outdoor fireplace and barbeque. The production facilities may be toured by appointment.

9150 Los Amigos Road
Windsor, CA 95492
(707) 838-9466

HOURS: 10 A.M.–5 P.M. Thursday–Sunday
TASTINGS: Yes
TOURS: By appointment
PICNIC AREA: Yes
RETAIL SALES: Yes
DIRECTIONS: From Highway 101, take Windsor exit, east to Lakewood, turn left; left at Brooks to winery drive.
VINTNER'S CHOICE: Chardonnay

Field Stone Winery

Healdsburg

Unlike most conventional wineries built from the ground up, Field Stone was built from the ground down. The late Wallace Johnson chose a natural, oak-studded knoll on his ranch and in the mid-1970s proceeded to carve out a long, narrow slice of earth.

After lining the walls with concrete and building a ceiling, workers redistributed soil over the bunker, returning the knoll to a reasonable facsimile of its former self. Field stone used to construct the facade was unearthed during excavation. This intriguing underground facility is said to be the only known winery of its kind to be built in California since 1900.

Wallace, an inventor of portable aluminum scaffolding, purchased the property in 1955 to pursue an interest in raising purebred cattle. However, after soil tests a few years later showed the ranch to be well suited to grapevines, Redwood Hereford Ranch evolved into Redwood Ranch and Vineyards. Construction of Field Stone came on the heels of an auspicious planting effort that began in the mid-sixties.

Unfortunately, the rancher-turned-vinter lived to see few crushes at Field Stone. Wallace died in 1979, and the winery passed to his daughter, Katrina, and son-in-law, Dr. John Staten.

Although Katrina had become familiar with the business while serving for many years as secretary-treasurer for her father, John was pursuing an unrelated career in theological education.

Redirecting his efforts, he eagerly set out to earn his new title of vintner and general manager. Field Stone has during the past few years also utilized the talents of consulting enologist Andre Tchelistcheff and winemaker James Thomson.

The efficient winery, bulging with modern tanks and equipment, is open for tours by appointment. Visitors will catch a glimpse of the production area on the way to the redwood-panelled tasting room, which is open daily. A number of tree-shaded picnic tables are scattered about the winery grounds.

FIELD STONE
ESTATE 1982 BOTTLED
SPRING-CABERNET
ALEXANDER VALLEY
GROWN, PRODUCED AND BOTTLED BY
REDWOOD RANCH AND VINEYARD • HEALDSBURG, CA
RESIDUAL SUGAR 1.5% • ALCOHOL 12.2% BY VOLUME

10075 Highway 128
Healdsburg, CA 95448
(707) 433-7266

HOURS: 10 A.M.–5 P.M. daily; closed
   Christmas and New Year's
TASTINGS: Yes
TOURS: By appointment
PICNIC AREA: Yes
RETAIL SALES: Yes
DIRECTIONS: Near intersection of Highway
   128 and Chalk Hill Road.
VINTNER'S CHOICE: Cabernet Sauvignon

Alexander Valley Vineyards

Healdsburg

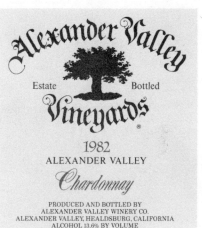

Wine grapes represent only one of myriad crops that have flourished on the estate now known as Alexander Valley Vineyards. In the 1840s Cyrus Alexander directed the establishment of a vast agricultural tract that included fruit trees, vegetable gardens, wheat fields, hops, and cattle and sheep ranches.

Recruited by landowner Henry Fitch to open the virgin northern section of his 300,000-acre Sotoyome Grant, Alexander became the first European settler of the valley that now bears his name.

After outgrowing his modest adobe, Alexander constructed an ornate ranch house in 1848. The homesite and several hundred acres remained in the Alexander family until 1963 when Los Angeles manufacturing company executive Harry Wetzel, Jr., and a friend purchased the old home along with some land and set about planting vineyards. By 1973, the estate had grown to 240 acres.

Wetzel's son, Harry (Hank) III, and daughter, Katie Wetzel-Murphy, run the business from an early California–style winery situated on a hillside a stone's throw from the restored Alexander homestead. The dark-stained, board and batten tasting room and offices sit atop the cellar, whose walls were fashioned from adobe.

Visitors may sample Alexander Valley's estate-bottled wines (ask about their popular Sin Zin) in the antique-furnished tasting room or soak up countryside views from the veranda.

8644 Highway 128
Healdsburg, CA 95448
(707) 433-7209

HOURS: 10 A.M.–5 P.M. daily; except major holidays
TASTINGS: Yes
TOURS: By appointment
PICNIC AREA: Yes
RETAIL SALES: Yes
DIRECTIONS: From Highway 101, east on Dry Creek Road, left on Healdsburg Avenue (becomes Alexander Valley Road), right on Highway 128 to winery drive.
VINTNER'S CHOICE: Chardonnay

J. Pedroncelli Winery

Geyserville

Second generation winemakers John and Jim Pedroncelli learned the trade from their father, John Sr., who in 1927 bought the winery that bears the family name.

The elder Pedroncelli began by selling grapes, later making bulk wine. He cultivated the vines throughout Prohibition and sold field-mixed grapes to home winemakers. John began to bottle under his own name by the 1940s.

His sons were introduced to the winemaker's way of life as youngsters, pulling weeds and plowing the vineyards. John Jr. was named winemaker in 1948, and a few years later Jim took over the business aspects of the winery. Ownership passed to the siblings by 1963.

Pedroncelli's somewhat compact appearance is a bit deceiving, as some 125,000 gallons are produced here each year. Tasting takes place at a bar on a cement floor at one end of a large concrete block warehouse. Among the nearly dozen varietals available at Pedroncelli is Zinfandel Rosé, a longtime favorite made from 100 percent Zinfandel grapes.

The Pedroncellis were drawing plans for a new tasting room when I visited the winery. Construction was expected to begin by the spring of 1985.

1220 Canyon Road
Geyserville, CA 95441
(707) 857-3531

HOURS: 10 A.M.–5 P.M. daily; closed major
   holidays
TASTINGS: Yes
TOURS: By appointment
PICNIC AREA: No
RETAIL SALES: Yes
DIRECTIONS: One mile west of Highway
   101 on Canyon Road.
VINTNER'S CHOICE: Zinfandel

Cordtz Brothers Cellars

Cloverdale

Tiny crawl holes are among few clues to the true origins of the unusual cellars and tasting area of Cordtz Brothers Cellars. The small concrete rooms which these days are filled with barrels are actually a series of outdated fermentors that once held thousands of gallons of wine.

Rather than abandon the tanks, David Cordtz carved doorways out of thick concrete and created a maze of "wine caves" where a constant cool temperature provides a choice spot for barrel aging. One of the 12,000-gallon tanks serves as a tasting room.

The business was known originally as the Hollis Black Winery, a medium-sized bulk wine producer that went out of business in the late 1960s. While the property is still held by David Black—his family has owned the winery for over 100 years—Cordtz leased the facility and established Cordtz Brothers Cellars in 1979. (Incidentally, there are no other Cordtz brothers involved in the operation.)

The winery consists primarily of two large buildings: an old barn built in 1906 and the newer concrete tank facility built in 1945. The two structures are connected by a courtyard shaded by a 250-year-old oak tree.

Unlike Hollis Black, which made its wine in bulk, David Cordtz produces his vintages in smaller quantities. Annual production ranges from 10,000 to 12,000 cases. Known primarily for Zinfandel, Cordtz Brothers Cellars makes Gewurztraminer, Sauvignon Blanc, Cabernet Sauvignon, Chardonnay, Muscat Blanc, Fume Blanc, Premium Red, and a concoction called Mama Tasca's Carignane.

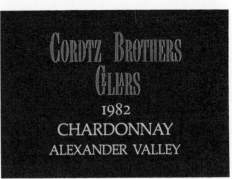

CORDTZ BROTHERS CELLARS
1982
CHARDONNAY
ALEXANDER VALLEY

28237 River Road
Cloverdale, CA 95425
(707) 894-5245

HOURS: 10 A.M.–4 P.M. daily
TASTINGS: Yes
TOURS: Yes, informal
PICNIC AREA: Yes
RETAIL SALES: Yes
DIRECTIONS: From downtown Cloverdale, east on First Street, cross Russian River, and south on River Road.
VINTNER'S CHOICE: Zinfandel

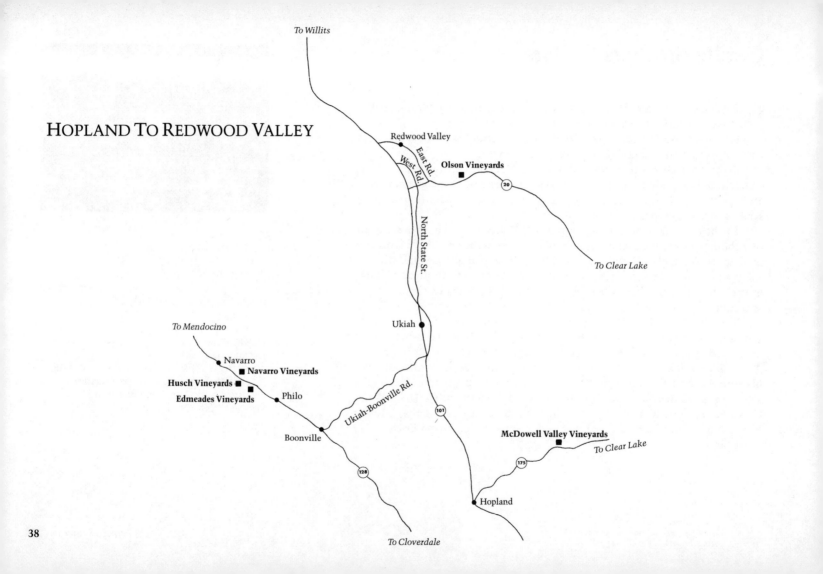

HOPLAND TO REDWOOD VALLEY

To Willits

Redwood Valley

East Rd.

West Rd.

Olson Vineyards

20

North State St.

To Clear Lake

Ukiah

To Mendocino

Navarro

Navarro Vineyards

Husch Vineyards

Edmeades Vineyards

Philo

Ukiah-Boonville Rd.

101

Boonville

McDowell Valley Vineyards

To Clear Lake

175

128

Hopland

38

To Cloverdale

McDowell Valley Vineyards

Hopland

Having learned in advance of my visit that McDowell Valley Vineyards held the distinction of being California's first solar winery, I visualized a makeshift building with a couple of unsightly solar panels stuck to the roof.

Contrary to my preconceptions, the facility revealed itself to be a handsome showplace of contemporary energy conservation and one of the most impressive small winemaking operations in the state, if not the nation.

An imposing sight even from the highway some distance away, the winery is particularly awe inspiring up close. The sprawling building is an artful arrangement of berms, beams, solar cells, decks, and windows nestled amongst 360 acres of vines, some of which are more than a half-century old.

McDowell Valley's recent designation as a distinct grape-growing appellation was the culmination of efforts by owners Karen and Richard Keehn, who documented the unique climatic and soil qualities here after establishing their winery in 1979.

The ground floor of the building, partially concealed behind a cooling earthen berm, holds a series of production, storage, fermentation, and bottling chambers. The second floor houses the tasting room, laboratory, catering kitchen, offices, and picnic decks. An expansive tasting room, which contains a baby grand piano for special events, is the centerpiece of the winery.

The facility's mechanical solar equipment includes 600 square feet of solar collectors, a complex water circulation system, and heat exchangers.

The more subtle passive elements—such as double-paned windows, skylights, and berms—serve to enhance not only the energy self-sufficiency of the building but its sleek appearance as well.

McDowell recently joined the ranks of wineries that have opened tasting rooms in Hopland. While many tasters will be content to sample McDowell wines in this convenient setting, it's well worth the extra few miles to see the real thing.

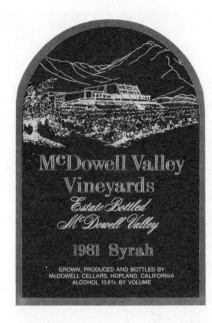

3811 Highway 175
Hopland, CA 95449
(707) 744-1053

HOURS: 10 A.M.–5 P.M. daily
TASTINGS: Yes
TOURS: Weekends at 11 A.M. and 2 P.M.
PICNIC AREA: Yes
RETAIL SALES: Yes
DIRECTIONS: From Hopland, east on Highway 175, 4 miles to winery sign.
VINTNER'S CHOICE: Syrah

Olson Vineyards

Redwood Valley

First-time visitors who make the ten-minute trek up into the hills outside of Ukiah for the sole purpose of sampling the wines of Olson Vineyards are treated to an unexpected bonus. The Olsons serve their wine with a view that any other vintner would be hard pressed to match. The family home, which houses the tasting room, is situated on benchland overlooking Lake Mendocino and Redwood Valley.

Don Olson, a transplanted Los Angeles electronic engineer, moved his wife, Nancy, and son, Dave, north to this site in 1971. The father-son winemaking team released the first Olson label vintage in 1983. Most of their grapes had previously been sold to Fetzer Winery.

The Olson establishment is a modest one. A wood-sided building next to the home shelters much of the operation. The crusher sits under an eave on the far side of the building.

Although the pleasing view from the tasting room isn't for sale, it is for rent. An adjacent lakeview suite of downstairs rooms and a private deck are available to overnight guests on a bed-and-breakfast lodging plan. For those intending a shorter visit, the Olsons have set up picnic tables in their backyard, which also overlooks the lake.

OLSON
VINEYARDS

1983

MENDOCINO COUNTY
FUME BLANC
(SAUVIGNON BLANC)

Produced and bottled by OLSON VINEYARDS
Redwood Valley, California, U.S.A. Alcohol 14.1% by volume

3620 Road B
Redwood Valley, CA 95470
(707) 485-7523

HOURS: 10 A.M.–5 P.M. Thursday–Monday
TASTINGS: Yes
TOURS: Yes
PICNIC AREA: Yes
RETAIL SALES: Yes
DIRECTIONS: From Highway 101, east on Highway 20, north on Road A, then east on Road B.
VINTNER'S CHOICE: Special Reserve Zinfandel and Chardonnay

44 *Navarro*

Navarro Vineyards

Philo

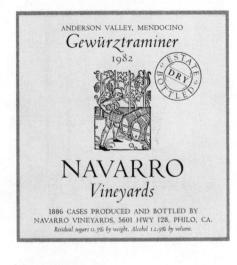

Ted Bennett, founder of the Pacific Stereo chain, left the Bay Area in 1975 with his wife, Deborah Cahn, to establish Navarro Vineyards, a quaint winemaking operation in Anderson Valley just north of Philo.

If the Navarro name is unfamiliar, it's probably because you'll not find the product in more than ten stores. About 80 percent of Navarro's 10,000 annual cases are sold from the tasting room.

The winery lures its potential customers with a distinctively rustic tasting room whose arched windows and glass doors offer views of surrounding flowers and vines. An attached deck holds umbrella-shaded picnic tables.

Other similarly styled buildings on the property include the owners' home, which used to be a barn, and a small winery built around some old oak trees. Those who make prior arrangements with Ted and Deborah may tour the production and aging facilities.

Navarro produces estate-bottled Gewurztraminer, Chardonnay, and Pinot Noir. Small lots of grapes from other Mendocino County vineyards are used to make White Riesling, Sauvignon Blanc, and an Edelwicker white table wine.

5601 Highway 128
Philo, CA 95466
(707) 895-3686

HOURS: 10 A.M.–5 P.M. in winter; 10 A.M.–
  6 P.M. in summer
TASTINGS: Yes
TOURS: By appointment
PICNIC AREA: Yes
RETAIL SALES: Yes
DIRECTIONS: Between Navarro and Philo
  on Highway 128.
VINTNER'S CHOICE: Gewurztraminer

Edmeades Vineyards

Philo

As the proprietor of one of scores of small wineries launched in California during the 1970s, Deron Edmeades thought long and hard about how to catch the attention of wine afficionados. He found the answer in proprietary wines that convey the distinctive character of the Anderson Valley, situated near the Mendocino coast.

The first was Rain Wine, created in 1975. Subsequent harvests produced Opal and even Whale Wine, some proceeds from which are contributed to marine preservation efforts. Several varietals complement the Edmeades roster.

Winemaking has been underway at Edmeades since 1972, but grape-growing began on the property in the early 1960s when Deron's father, Donald, a Southern California physician, bought the property. From Dr. Edmeades' planting of Anderson Valley's first post-Prohibition varietal wine grapes until his death in 1972, grapes from the ranch were sold to Parducci Winery.

The Edmeades tasting room is within the wooden walls of a converted garage adjacent to the ranch house. A summer concert series is held in the small apple orchard behind the winery.

1983
Mendocino
Dry White Pinot Noir
OPAL

Edmeades Vineyards

Produced and bottled by Edmeades Vineyards,
Philo, Anderson Valley,
Mendocino County, California
Alcohol 11.3% by volume

5500 Highway 128
Philo, CA 95466
(707) 895-3232

HOURS: 11 A.M.–5 P.M. in winter; 10 A.M.–
6 P.M. in summer
TASTINGS: Yes
TOURS: By appointment
PICNIC AREA: Yes
RETAIL SALES: Yes
DIRECTIONS: North of Philo near
Greenwood Road on Highway 128.
VINTNER'S CHOICE: DuPratt Zinfandel

48 *Husch*

Husch Vineyards

Philo

Husch is the oldest of the smattering of small wineries that occupy Mendocino County's cool Anderson Valley. While it is the elder, Husch is by no means old. Wilton and Gretchen Husch bonded the operation in 1971.

Hugo Oswald and his family, who have grown grapes in Mendocino County for more than two decades, now own Husch, a 10,000 case-per-year winery situated between Navarro and Philo on Highway 128.

"Unadorned rustic" is how the Oswalds describe their facilities, which consist of a small, wood-frame winery and an old granary. This small building now functions as a tasting room. Picnic tables are available for visitors.

"La Ribera," the Oswald ranch near Ukiah, supplies a good portion of the winery's grapes. It is the Husch vineyard, however, that earned for the winery a bit of international fame. The 1983 estate-bottled Gewurztraminer was among a few California wines to accompany President Ronald Reagan on his trip to China in 1984. The Husch wine was served at a state dinner in Beijing in honor of People's Republic Premier Zhao Ziyang. Quite an honor for a wine that retailed at the time for just over six dollars per bottle.

HUSCH

Anderson Valley

Gewurztraminer

Estate 1983 Bottled

*Grown, produced and bottled by the H.A. Oswald family
Anderson Valley, Philo, California*

ALCOHOL 12.0% BY VOLUME, RESIDUAL SUGAR 1.2% BY WEIGHT.

4900 Star Route, Highway 128
Philo, CA 95466
(707) 895-3216

HOURS: 10 A.M.–5 P.M. in winter; 10 A.M.–6 P.M. in summer
TASTINGS: Yes
TOURS: By appointment
PICNIC AREA: Yes
RETAIL SALES: Yes
DIRECTIONS: Between Navarro and Philo on Highway 128.
VINTNER'S CHOICE: Chardonnay

THE NAPA VALLEY REGION

Leave the Crowds Behind

P sst! It's still possible to enjoy a leisurely tour of Napa Valley area wineries. While the weekend congestion along narrow Highway 29 can often rival Los Angeles rush-hour traffic, a little planning and a sense of adventure will take you into a wonderland overlooked by all but the most seasoned winery enthusiasts.

The tours outlined in the following pages cover a wide area—from Green Valley, near the junction of Highways 80 and 680, all the way to Calistoga. In between are pleasant mountain roads and panoramic vistas that most wine country visitors pass up in favor of the more famous establishments on the valley floor.

The backroads of this region, while free of heavy traffic, are remarkably rich in wineries. Many have operated in relative obscurity for decades, their stately stone cellars visibly great with age. Nichelini Vineyards, for example, has been in the same family since the mining days of the nineteenth century.

Others, like Chateau de Leu near Suisun in tiny Green Valley, are more recent additions to this world-famous countryside.

There is a common denominator, however. Each of these backroad operations welcomes visitors in an unhurried, intimate atmosphere that has all but disappeared from many of the larger wineries of Napa Valley. Just don't tell too many people.

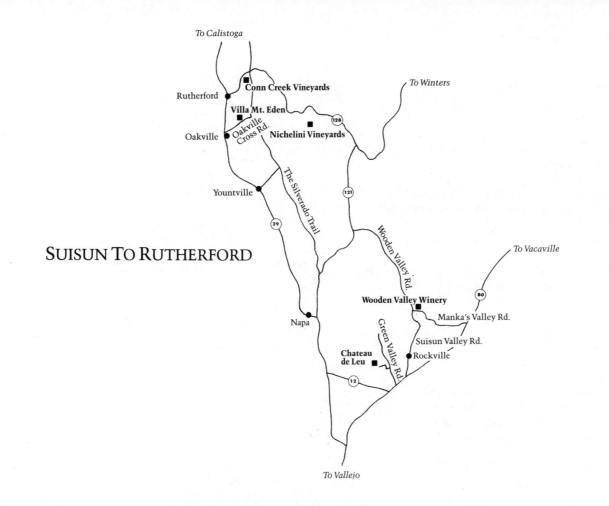

To Calistoga

Conn Creek Vineyards

Rutherford

Villa Mt. Eden

To Winters

Oakville

Oakville Cross Rd.

128

Nichelini Vineyards

The Silverado Trail

Yountville

121

29

To Vacaville

SUISUN TO RUTHERFORD

Wooden Valley Rd.

80

Wooden Valley Winery

Manka's Valley Rd.

Napa

Green Valley Rd.

Suisun Valley Rd.

Chateau de Leu

Rockville

12

To Vallejo

Wooden Valley Winery

Suisun

During my visit to the Lanza family winery on Suisun Valley Road, a steady stream of customers pulled in to load their vehicles with supplies of Wooden Valley wines. That scene sufficiently explained the family's unusual independence. Other than the winery itself, a handful of restaurants are the only places one can order the Lanza product.

Wooden Valley Winery is a nondescript collection of older buildings which includes the home of the proprietors, Mario and Lena Lanza. Their son Richard is also a partner. The Lanzas bought Wooden Valley and more than 150 acres of vineyard from some friends back in the 1950s. In those days Suisun Valley Road was known as Wooden Valley Road, hence the name.

The family receives visitors at a long L-shaped bar in the spacious tasting room. The winery needs the space to display its wares. On my visit, the roster listed more than forty varieties. In addition to a traditional list of varietals, Wooden Valley produces Pink Chateau, Malvasia Bianca, four types of sherry, vermouth, and champagne. The Lanzas bottle under the Wooden Valley, Solano, and Mario Lanza labels.

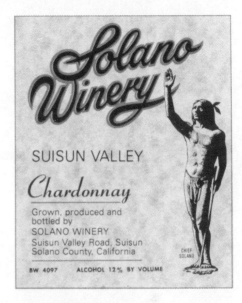

4756 Suisun Valley Road
Suisun, CA 94585
(707) 864-0730

HOURS: 9 A.M.–5 P.M. Tuesday–Sunday
TASTINGS: Yes
TOURS: No
PICNIC AREA: Yes
RETAIL SALES: Yes
DIRECTIONS: From Interstate 80 at Cordelia, north on Suisun Valley Road for 4.5 miles.

Chateau de Leu

Green Valley–Suisun

A full century elapsed between the first plantings and the establishment of a winery in Green Valley, a tiny viticultural area where grapes have grown since 1882. The father and son team of Ben Volkhardt Jr. and Ben III built Chateau de Leu in 1982 on land that has been owned by the family since the 1950s.

The family decided to create wines under their own label in 1981, after several years of selling grapes to other vintners. The result is an imposing French Tudor–style chateau designed to produce up to 25,000 cases per year.

The modern winery houses ten large temperature-controlled stainless steel fermentation tanks and scores of French Limousin barrels. Chateau de Leu also utilizes a field crusher that yields a thousand gallons per cycle.

Tours are by appointment, but a tasting room is open daily. This handsome public room is located on the second level and features a deck from which visitors can view Green Valley.

The four-square-mile basin gives way to mountains in all directions but south, allowing marine air off San Francisco Bay to interact with the region's own climatic conditions, thus producing grapes with a unique set of characteristics. Some 400 acres of Green Valley are presently planted to grapes.

1635 West Mason Road
Green Valley–Suisun, CA 94585
(707) 864-1517

HOURS: 11 A.M.–4:30 P.M. daily
TASTINGS: Yes
TOURS: By appointment
PICNIC AREA: Yes
RETAIL SALES: Yes
DIRECTIONS: Leave Interstate 80 at the Green Valley Road exit, north on Green Valley Road for 2 miles, left on West Mason, 1 mile to winery.
VINTNER'S CHOICE: Chardonnay

Nichelini Vineyard

St. Helena

Antone Nichelini was among the group of Italian immigrants that worked the magnesite mines in the hills above Napa during the nineteenth century. When mining activity slowed, Nichelini homesteaded some land and, in 1890, built a modest sandstone winery topped by a house in which he raised his family.

The operation thrived until Prohibition, during which Nichelini maintained a clandestine winemaking business. Although Repeal signaled the reopening of wineries throughout the state, a bootlegging conviction precluded Antone from securing a license. His son Jim obtained the necessary permits and helped to keep the vineyards going through the ensuing ups and downs of the industry. When the price of whole grapes took a dive in the mid-1940s, seventeen-year-old Jim Jr. was recruited to help his father increase the production of wine.

Although Antone and Jim Sr. died several years ago, their contributions to the property are still evident. The original homesteaders' cabin has been preserved, as has an old Roman press, which was retired in the 1950s. Jim Jr. has also held on to numerous other pieces of antiquated equipment and assorted odds and ends which are displayed in the winery.

While Jim runs primarily a one-man show much of the year, daughter Joann drives up on occasional weekends to help her dad, thus carrying on a familiar story that has kept Nichelini alive for four generations.

2349 Lower Chiles Valley Road
St. Helena, CA 94574
(707) 963-3357

HOURS: 10 A.M.–6 P.M. Saturday and Sunday; and by appointment
TASTINGS: Yes
TOURS: Yes, self-guided
PICNIC AREA: Yes
RETAIL SALES: Yes
DIRECTIONS: Eleven miles east of Highway 29 on Highway 128.
VINTNER'S CHOICE: Zinfandel

Conn Creek

St. Helena

In a valley known for its many distinctive stone cellars, Conn Creek was undoubtedly viewed as somewhat of a maverick when construction of the building began along the Silverado Trail in 1979. After outgrowing a ninety-year-old facility, winery owners Bill and Kathy Collins chose a completely different style for their new 15,000 square-foot winery. Instead of stone, the couple opted for a Styrofoam-type material. While it's not readily apparent, Conn Creek is built of lightweight foam blocks stacked between steel beams and sprayed with Gunite. The energy efficient design, unique in 1979, has since become a model for other wineries.

The label predates the present building by several years. The Collinses, who have been growing grapes in the Napa Valley for some time, founded the winery in 1974, utilizing other local facilities before building their own. More than half of the annual grape crop comes from Napa Valley vineyards owned by Bill and Kathy. Two other families also hold interest in the winery, which produces Cabernet Sauvignon, Chardonnay, and Zinfandel.

Much of the internal workings of the operation may be viewed from a window in an upstairs public room. Informal tastings are conducted here at a table and chairs.

The vineyard scene that graces the Conn Creek label is the work of noted California artist and author Earl Thollander, a resident of Napa Valley.

8711 Silverado Trail
St. Helena, CA 94574
(707) 963-9100

HOURS: By appointment
TASTINGS: By appointment
TOURS: By appointment
PICNIC AREA: No
RETAIL SALES: By appointment
DIRECTIONS: Intersection of Highway 128 and the Silverado Trail.
VINTNER'S CHOICE: Cabernet Sauvignon

62 *Villa Mt. Eden*

Villa Mt. Eden

Oakville

Villa Mt. Eden has operated under various names on a century-old Napa Valley wine estate, but has only in recent years begun to shed some of its mystery. The winery, while still maintaining a relatively low profile, has opened a tasting room for valley visitors and invites tours on a call-ahead basis.

The estate belongs to James McWilliams and his wife, Anne, granddaughter of Bank of America founder A. P. Giannini. The McWilliamses, who took over in 1970, obviously take pride in the estate, which is lovingly maintained.

The winery buildings, one of which dates back to 1882, are painted white with blue trim. A rambling, 1920s-era Mediterranean-style villa serves as a weekend and summer retreat for the owners, who make their permanent home in San Francisco.

The several buildings, including an old pump house, form a tight cluster under an ancient eucalyptus tree. Tastings take place near the public entrance in a small converted home that also serves as an office. Clark Gable and Carole Lombard reportedly spent time at the little house while filming a movie on the property.

The eighty-seven acres of vines that encircle the winery extend to the Silverado Trail. The owners concentrate their efforts on Cabernet Sauvignon, Chardonnay, and Chenin Blanc.

Mt. Eden Ranch
P.O. Box 147
Oakville, CA 94562
(707) 944-8431

HOURS: 10 A.M.–4 P.M. daily; closed major holidays
TASTINGS: Yes
TOURS: By appointment
PICNIC AREA: Yes
RETAIL SALES: Yes
DIRECTIONS: On north side of Oakville crossing, between the Silverado Trail and Highway 29.
VINTNER'S CHOICE: Cabernet Sauvignon

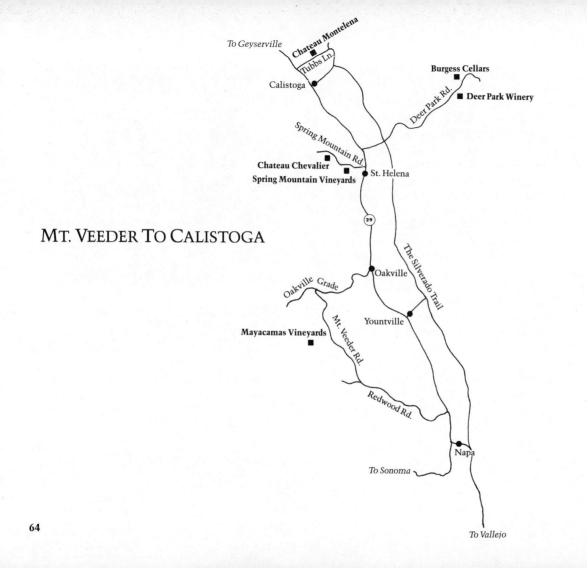

MT. VEEDER TO CALISTOGA

To Geyserville

Chateau Montelena

Tubbs Ln.

Calistoga

Burgess Cellars

Deer Park Rd.

Deer Park Winery

Spring Mountain Rd.

Chateau Chevalier

Spring Mountain Vineyards

St. Helena

29

Oakville

The Silverado Trail

Oakville Grade

Yountville

Mt. Veeder Rd.

Mayacamas Vineyards

Redwood Rd.

Napa

To Sonoma

To Vallejo

Mayacamas Vineyards

Napa

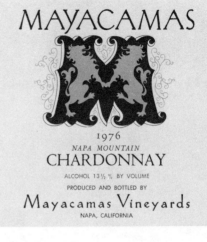

One of the few California wineries whose vines are dusted with winter snows, Mayacamas Vineyards sits high in the mountains above the bustle of Napa and Sonoma valleys. The winery and vineyards are perched on an ancient volcanic ledge whose rich soil has fed the vines since German-born sword engraver John Fisher established his winemaking operation here in the late 1800s.

Bob and Nonie Travers are the present owners. The couple bought Mayacamas in 1968 after Bob left his job as a stock analyst in San Francisco. With the exception of the addition of a cellar and some new vines, Bob has done little to alter the rustic appearance of Mayacamas. Built into a hillside to take advantage of gravity, before the era of electric pumps, the old winery houses its crusher and press on the uppermost level. From there the juices flow into the original concrete-lined fermentation tanks. The Cabernets are aged in large American oak and small French oak barrels in the old stone-walled cellar below. While the Chardonnay is ready for consumption after three years of aging, patience is the key to enjoying Mayacamas reds. Bob uses winemaking techniques that give his Cabernets longevity and require a lengthier maturing time. "Prime enjoyment of our 1979 Cabernet Sauvignon should come in the last few years of this century and the first few of the next," he says. "We make red wine this way primarily, of course, to test the patience and restraint of our customers."

For those unwilling to wait until the year 2000 to taste the fruits of Mayacamas, the Traverses each year release a number of cases from a decade or so earlier.

Patience is also required of those who venture up the mountain roads to the winery. After navigating the eight or so miles of winding roads from Napa on the valley floor, visitors—and their vehicles—must endure a mile-long dirt driveway before reaching Mayacamas.

1155 Lokoya Road
Napa, CA 94558
(707) 224-4030

HOURS: By appointment
TASTINGS: No
TOURS: Monday and Wednesday at 10 A.M., Friday at 2 P.M.; by appointment
PICNIC AREA: No
RETAIL SALES: By appointment
DIRECTIONS: Leave Highway 29 at Redwood Road, right on Mt. Veeder, left on Lokoya, left on dirt road at sign to winery.
VINTNER'S CHOICE: Cabernet Sauvignon

Spring Mountain Vineyards

St. Helena

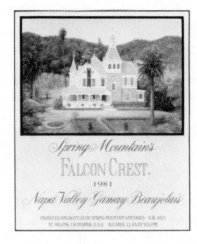

Wineries that are fortunate enough to earn a loyal following do so for their particular wares. One Napa Valley exception, however, is Spring Mountain Vineyard, which has come by its reputation not so much for its fine wines but for the manor house that has been seen by millions of television viewers.

Those who are not devotees of prime-time soap opera will probably be confused by all the fuss over a house. Followers of *Falcon Crest*, on the other hand, drive up by the hundreds each week to gawk at the stately Victorian that is featured in opening scenes of the T.V. show. On my visit to the estate, attention was focused not on the beautiful winery but on the adjacent home. One visitor gestured toward the residence and asked me if that was "the house."

First-time visitors will discover that the home is not included on the tour. This isn't a cause for disappointment, since the winery itself is one of the most handsome to be found in the region.

The above-ground portion of Spring Mountain is fairly new, built by founder Michael Robbins in 1976 in a grand style similar to that of his Victorian residence a few hundred yards away. Inside are a richly appointed tasting room and upstairs offices. Stained glass, much of it designed and constructed by Robbins, is used generously throughout the public areas. A huge chandelier, which originally hung in the mansion, is now a fixture of the winery. A nice view of "the house" from the tasting area is framed by an arched window with etchings of grapevines.

Wines are aged in a long, century-old tunnel that was dug into the hillside behind the facility. An adjacent area is reserved for fermentation tanks.

In addition to the Spring Mountain label, the winery bottles a newer selection of wines under the name *Falcon Crest*. These wines, while not up to the premium standards of the Spring Mountain vintages, are nonetheless big sellers—for obvious reasons.

2805 Spring Mountain Road
St. Helena, CA 94574
(707) 963-5233

HOURS: 10 A.M.–4 P.M. daily
TASTINGS: Yes
TOURS: 10:30 A.M. and 2:30 P.M., by appointment
PICNIC AREA: No
RETAIL SALES: Yes
DIRECTIONS: From Highway 29 in St. Helena, west on Madrona, right on Spring Mountain Road for 1 mile to white gate and stone wall.
VINTNER'S CHOICE: Cabernet Sauvignon and Chardonnay

70 *Chateau Chevalier*

Chateau Chevalier

St. Helena

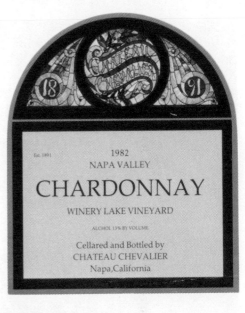

Of the myriad wineries scattered about the Napa Valley, Chateau Chevalier is one of the most striking—and one of the least known.

A businessman by the name of Chevalier settled this hidden, wooded site on the outskirts of St. Helena before the turn of the century. Here he established an enchanting estate with lush gardens, vineyards, and a bold, stone-walled winery whose second level was fitted with turrets and other architectural flourishes.

Although Chateau Chevalier produced wines for several years, the upper level of the winery was later converted to a residence and production ceased. Winemaking resumed in the mid-1970s after replanting of the vineyards.

When I visited Chateau Chevalier, new owners Gil and John Nickel, proprietors of Far Niente Winery, hadn't quite settled in and were still finalizing their plans for continuing restoration efforts at the historic manor. Even the new wine roster had yet to be established.

This classic winery may be visited by appointment only. The owners, who value their privacy, will provide directions over the phone to the unmarked lane.

P.O. Box 991
St. Helena, CA 94574
(707) 963-2342

HOURS: By appointment
TASTINGS: By appointment
TOURS: By appointment
PICNIC AREA: No
RETAIL SALES: Yes
DIRECTIONS: Call for an appointment and directions.

Deer Park Winery
Deer Park

It is said that the Napa Valley is second only to Disneyland as California's biggest tourist attraction. You could fool David and Kinta Clark, however. Highway 29 traffic may be bumper to bumper most weekends, but the road up to the Clarks' little Deer Park Winery is usually pretty quiet.

Those who do venture out of St. Helena and are able to locate the winery will not be disappointed. The centerpiece at Deer Park is a rustic, century-old cellar that turns out wines in small amounts—only about 5,000 cases per year.

David is both winemaker and vineyard tender. When I visited Deer Park he was in the process of carving soil for additional vines, which would bring the total productive acreage to about six. The remaining forty or so acres on the property consist primarily of rocks, hills, and trees—nice to look at, but not conducive to cultivation.

David came by his winemaking talents through apprenticeships at Cuvaison and Clos du Val. He and his wife, Kinta, along with David's sister and brother-in-law, Lila and Bob Knapp, bought Deer Park in 1979, resuming a tradition of winemaking that began in 1891 on the estate.

Like many old wineries built into hillsides, Deer Park was set up to operate on a gravity-flow basis. In the old days, wagons would unload the grapes at the top of the hill at the upper part of the building where crushing took place. Gravity carried the juices downhill to fermentation and aging cooperage.

Although more modern means are used these days, David, for sentimental reasons, has held on to much of the equipment from Deer Park's earlier years.

In addition to welcoming guests for winery tours, Deer Park offers overnight accommodations. The owners have converted a guest cottage, part of which was once an old railroad station, to a bed and breakfast cottage.

Although the name indicates otherwise, the Clarks say there are no deer at Deer Park. The way David tells it, the moniker was apparently conceived by a 1920s-era owner who wanted to shake any unpleasant association of his winery with the country byway that ends at the property—Sanitarium Road.

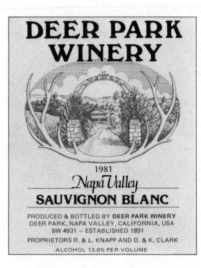

1000 Dear Park Road
Deer Park, CA 94576
(707) 963-5411

HOURS: 9 A.M.–4 P.M., daily, by appointment
TASTINGS: By appointment
TOURS: By appointment
PICNIC AREA: Yes, by appointment
RETAIL SALES: Yes
DIRECTIONS: From Highway 29 north of St. Helena, east on Deer Park Road for 3.5 miles to winery.
VINTNER'S CHOICE: Sauvignon Blanc (1981)

Burgess Cellars

St. Helena

Burgess Cellars, while not on the list of wineries offering drop-in tastings, is worthy of a visit if for nothing else than a look at the fine old rock and wood frame winery—one of only a handful left in the region.

Tom and Linda Burgess passed up newer facilities in favor of this vintage property, originally homesteaded in the 1880s. It became Burgess Cellars in 1972.

Like neighboring Deer Park Winery, the Burgess Cellar was built before electricity on a sloping site to take advantage of the flow of gravity. Production and fermentation took place on the level above the stone-walled storage cellars.

In the early years the operation produced bulk wines for sale to the more substantial wineries in Napa Valley. Today, the Burgesses use grapes from their estate vineyards to produce small amounts of Zinfandel, Cabernet Franc, and Cabernet Sauvignon. Chardonnay is also bottled under the Burgess label.

Although the small winery may be toured only by appointment, the retail sales office is open daily from 10 A.M. to 4 P.M.

1108 Deer Park Road
St. Helena, CA 94575
(707) 963-4766

HOURS: 10 A.M.–4 P.M. daily
TASTINGS: By appointment
TOURS: By appointment
PICNIC AREA: No
RETAIL SALES: Yes
DIRECTIONS: From Highway 29, drive 3.4 miles on Deer Park Road to winery gate.
VINTNER'S CHOICE: Chardonnay

76 *Chateau Montelena*

Chateau Montelena

Calistoga

Divergent influences of Chinese and French architecture stand side by side at one of Napa Valley's oldest and most intriguing small wineries.

Chateau Montelena was built in 1882 by California State Senator and prominent Bay Area businessman Alfred Tubbs. In establishing his winery near the base of Mount St. Helena, Senator Tubbs called upon the design talents of an architect from France who created a building in the style of a French chateau. The medieval facade was fashioned from imported cut stone. The other walls—the winery is cut into the side of a hill—are as thick as twelve feet in certain places, providing an environment akin to a cave, perfect for making wine.

While the winery itself conjures up images of feudal Bordeaux, the adjacent grounds could have been lifted from a garden in Peking. Jade Lake, with its delicate tea houses, graceful bridges, and an old Chinese junk, was added to the property by the Yort Franks, later owners who in the late 1950s created a living reminder of their ancestral homeland of China.

The latest chapter in the Montelena story is being written by a partnership that took over in 1972. The new owners have preserved the architectural heritage of the winery and nurtured the gardens while carving a new reputation for their product. This winemaking renaissance is evidenced in part by framed menus from the White House which list Montelena wines. These hang in the tasting room along with other awards bestowed on the chateau's wines in recent years.

Chateau Montelena produces Cabernet Sauvignon, Chardonnay, Johannisberg Riesling, and Zinfandel.

1429 Tubbs Lane
Calistoga, CA 94515
(707) 942-5105

HOURS: 10 A.M.–4 P.M. daily
TASTINGS: Yes
TOURS: 11 A.M. and 2 P.M. by appointment
PICNIC AREA: By appointment
RETAIL SALES: Yes
DIRECTIONS: From Highway 29, west on Tubbs Lane to winery gate.
VINTNER'S CHOICE: Cabernet Sauvignon

THE CENTRAL COAST

Cruising the Coastal Byways

I f your visits to the Central Coast have been confined to the popular seaside resorts, you'll be surprised at the growing list of wineries operating along the backroads of this region. A day trip from Santa Cruz, Monterey, Carmel, or San Jose will introduce you to several enticing winemaking operations and some of the state's most beautiful countryside.

The coastal scenery is diverse as well. If your starting point is the Monterey Peninsula, you'll quickly exchange the cool coastal environs for the warmer climate of Carmel Valley. After winding eastward to the top of the mountains, the fertile Salinas Valley unfolds below.

This roller coaster tour culminates with a jaunt down the slope, a short hop across the valley floor, and a final ascent toward the Pinnacles National Monument above Soledad.

Equally impressive is the setting in and around Santa Cruz County, where golden beaches give way to redwood forests only a few miles inland.

If your tour route is Hecker Pass Road between Watsonville and Gilroy, be sure to include a visit to the less crowded wineries of the Uvas Valley. It is here that hospitable vintners like the Kirigin-Chargin (Kirigin Cellars) and the Parks (Sycamore Creek Vineyards) families practice the age-old art at two of the region's oldest and most charming wineries.

Free tour guides to Central Coast wineries are available from local chambers of commerce. For details, see the Grape Escapes section at the back of this book.

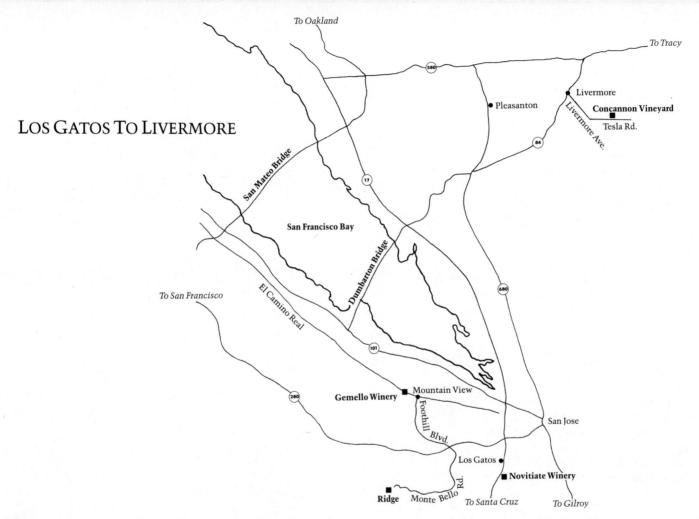

LOS GATOS TO LIVERMORE

To Oakland

To Tracy

580

Pleasanton

Livermore

Concannon Vineyard

Tesla Rd.

San Mateo Bridge

84

Livermore Ave.

17

San Francisco Bay

Dumbarton Bridge

To San Francisco

El Camino Real

680

101

280

Gemello Winery

Mountain View

Foothill Blvd.

San Jose

Los Gatos

Novitiate Winery

Ridge

Monte Bello Rd.

To Santa Cruz

To Gilroy

Novitiate Winery

Los Gatos

Novitiate, an ecclesiastical word meaning a place where a novice, or a beginner lives, is probably not the most accurate description of this venerable establishment. Hardly a newcomer, Novitiate has seen winemaking traditions handed down since 1888.

The winery, nestled above Los Gatos on the eastern slope of the Santa Cruz Mountains, was founded as a means of supporting young novices in training and of obtaining sacramental wines for celebrating Mass.

Commercial as well as church demand for the wines grew, and the winery moved to larger quarters in the 1890s. The old concrete structure survived the 1906 earthquake and a fire in 1934, and is still in use.

The popularity of Novitiate wines was triggered largely by the arrival of Brother Louis Olivier, a Frenchman who became winemaker here in 1890. It was Brother Louis who imported from France the select cuttings that yielded outstanding vintages over the ensuing years.

Until the 1960s, Novitiate produced 90 percent of its wine for sacramental purposes. Today, aperitif, dinner, and dessert wines account for more than half the winery's annual sales.

There have been other changes. No longer used for training, the facility housing Novitiate Winery is now called the Sacred Heart Jesuit Center, functioning as a retirement and retreat complex and administrative offices.

Tours of the winery lead visitors through a damp maze of century-old passageways and culminate in a more modern tasting room where wines as well as T-shirts and other gifts are sold.

P.O. Box 128
Los Gatos, CA 95030
(408) 354-6471

HOURS: 10 A.M.–4:30 P.M., daily
TASTINGS: Yes
TOURS: 1:30 and 2:30 P.M. Monday–
    Friday; 11 A.M. and 1 P.M. weekends
PICNIC AREA: Yes
RETAIL SALES: Yes
DIRECTIONS: From Main Street in Los
    Gatos, south on College Avenue to
    winery gate, up hill to winery.
VINTNER'S CHOICE: Black Muscat

Ridge

Cupertino

Looking north, the skyscrapers of San Francisco's financial district are often visible. Below, the high technology capital of the world sprawls along the valley floor. As I drank the view with a glass of Ridge Zinfandel, the name Paradox Ridge seemed more suitable for this winery.

Even though computers have made their way into this internationally famous winemaking establishment, the unpretentious ranch scene that greets visitors at Ridge stands in ultimate contrast to Silicon Valley, more than 2,000 feet below.

That's part of the tradition at Ridge, where the "old ways" apply to both aesthetics and winemaking. The winery actually exists in two parts. The lower site—formerly the Torres winery—houses offices, a tasting area, and case storage. The old Perrone Winery, a redwood and stone structure, is the actual production facility for Ridge wines and is not open to the public.

Ridge Vineyards is a relatively new name, originated in 1959 when four Stanford Research Institute scientists set up shop here, making wine with their families during spare moments. Ridge's reputation dates from the first release in 1962, but much of the winery's notoriety can be traced to the arrival of Paul Draper. The Stanford alumnus joined the operation as winemaker in 1969 after studying and practicing the trade in Italy, France, and Chile. Paul was among the first to popularize the claret-style Zinfandels that have since been widely emulated.

Ridge has fifty nonirrigated acres planted to grapes and makes purchases from various other vineyards whose appellations are noted on the label. Annual production fluctuates between 30,000 and 40,000 cases, with Cabernet Sauvignon representing about 40 percent of the total. In addition to Zinfandel, Ridge produces a small amount of Petite Sirah.

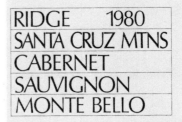

RIDGE 1980
SANTA CRUZ MTNS
CABERNET
SAUVIGNON
MONTE BELLO

100% CABERNET SAUVIGNON, MONTE BELLO VINEYARDS
SANTA CRUZ MOUNTAINS   ALCOHOL 12.4% BY VOLUME
PRODUCED AND BOTTLED BY RIDGE VINEYARDS, INC. BW 4488
17100 MONTE BELLO ROAD, P.O. BOX AI, CUPERTINO, CALIFORNIA

17100 Monte Bello Road
Cupertino, CA 95015
(408) 867-3233

HOURS: 11 A.M.–3 P.M. Saturday
TASTINGS: Yes
TOURS: No
PICNIC AREA: Yes
RETAIL SALES: Yes
DIRECTIONS: From Highway 280, south on Foothill Boulevard, right on Monte Bello Road for 4.4 miles to number 17100.
VINTNER'S CHOICE: Ridge Zinfandel

Gemello Winery

Mountain View

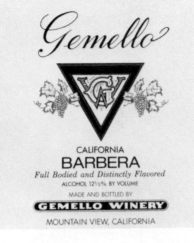

Upon visiting historic Gemello Winery in the midst of bustling Mountain View, guests often remark that the location is "a strange place for a winery." In truth, it's a strange place for a city, since Gemello was here long before the bowling alley, drive-in restaurant, and apartments that today squeeze the modest establishment. A house, tasting room/store and winery are all that remain of a once sprawling winemaking operation that included more than two dozen acres of vineyard.

Gemello was founded just after Repeal by John Gemello, a native of Italy's Piedemonte Region. Settling with his family on a ranch overlooking the valley, John set about making robust red wines in an oak-aged style that is observed to this day at the winery. The winemaker helped dig the cellar next to an old apricot drying room that was converted to a production facility.

John's son Mario took over some years later and operated the business until his retirement in 1978. There being no immediate family interest, crushing ceased, and much of the winery equipment was sold.

Several miles away in Half Moon Bay, however, John Gemello's grand-daughter, Sandy, and her husband, Paul Obester, were in the early stages of establishing Obester Winery. In 1982, Sandy and Paul stepped in to carry on the Gemello tradition, and production resumed, on a smaller scale. The winery today bottles less than 5,000 cases per year.

Tastings are conducted on one side of a counter in the Gemello Store next to the winery. The establishment also offers off-sale wine and liquor and serves other wines by the glass. Gemello has become well known for its bring-your-own-bottle event held every couple of months. Using the winery's vintage equipment, customers fill their own containers with special Gemello blends.

2003 El Camino Real
Mountain View, CA 94040
(415) 948-7723

HOURS: 11 A.M.–7 P.M. Tuesday-Thursday;
    11 A.M.–8 P.M. Friday; 9 A.M.–8 P.M.
    Saturday; 11 A.M.–5 P.M. Sunday
TASTINGS: Yes
TOURS: By appointment
PICNIC AREA: No
RETAIL SALES: Yes
DIRECTIONS: From Highway 101, take
    Rengstorff exit south; left at El Camino
    Real to winery drive.
VINTNER'S CHOICE: Cabernet Sauvignon
    and White Zinfandel

88 *Concannon*

Concannon Vineyard

Livermore

James Concannon's pioneering efforts in the western wine industry were largely the result of urgings from a San Francisco archbishop who needed a reliable source of sacramental wines for the Catholic Church. The Irish immigrant obliged by purchasing forty-seven acres in 1883, establishing what is today one of the state's oldest continuously operating wineries.

James transcended the original intention of his winery, becoming well known to others outside the church. In searching for other grape-growing locales, he later took his talents to Mexico and is widely credited with establishing that country's wine industry.

Joseph Concannon, one of the vintner's ten children, carried on after his father's death. Joseph's son, Jim, is president of Concannon today, although the business is owned by Distillers Corporation Unlimited. The winery still produces sacramental wines but is better known these days for such varieties as Sauvignon Blanc, Cabernet Sauvignon, Chardonnay, and Livermore Riesling. Concannon was the first American winery to make Petite Sirah, which was released in 1964.

A cavernous masonry facility that sits among vineland at the edge of Livermore, the winery makes admirable efforts to accommodate visitors. Tours are given four times daily, and the tasting room is open seven days a week. Concannon's well-maintained grounds include several picnic tables scattered about an expansive lawn.

ESTATE BOTTLED

SINCE 1883

Concannon
1978

LIVERMORE VALLEY
PETITE SIRAH

GROWN, PRODUCED & BOTTLED BY
CONCANNON VINEYARD, LIVERMORE,
CALIFORNIA, U.S.A., ALC. 12.5% BY VOL.

4590 Tesla Road
Livermore, CA 94550
(415) 447-3760

HOURS: 9 A.M.–5 P.M. weekdays; 10 A.M.–5 P.M. Saturday; 12–5 P.M. Sunday
TASTINGS: Yes
TOURS: Four times daily
PICNIC AREA: Yes
RETAIL SALES: Yes
DIRECTIONS: From Interstate 580 (east), take North Livermore Avenue and drive south 3 miles to winery.
VINTNER'S CHOICE: Petite Sirah

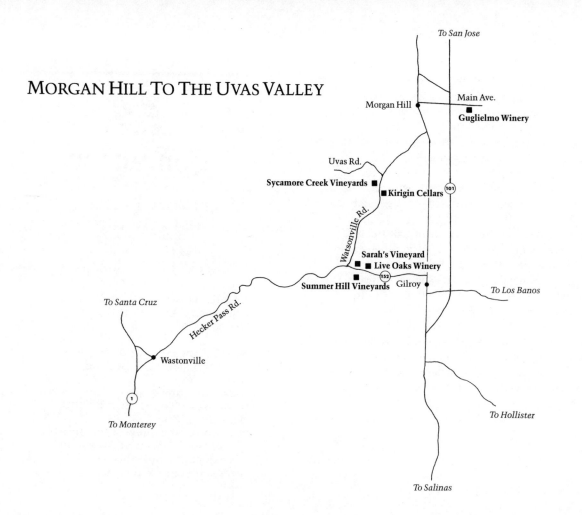

MORGAN HILL TO THE UVAS VALLEY

To San Jose

Main Ave.

Morgan Hill

Guglielmo Winery

Uvas Rd.

Sycamore Creek Vineyards ■

■ **Kirigin Cellars**

Watsonville Rd.

Sarah's Vineyard

■ **Live Oaks Winery**

Summer Hill Vineyards

Gilroy

To Los Banos

To Santa Cruz

Hecker Pass Rd.

Wastonville

To Monterey

To Hollister

To Salinas

Emilio Guglielmo Winery

Morgan Hill

It seemed only logical for George and Gene Guglielmo to follow their father's footsteps into the winemaking business. After all, there must be at least a trace of wine in their blood. Since Roman times, when Guglielmos made wine in Northern Italy, traditions have been passed from generation to generation.

The family history on this continent can be traced back three generations to Emilio Guglielmo's arrival in the Santa Clara Valley in the early 1900s. He worked for more than a dozen years to earn enough money to buy fifteen acres, build a home, and establish a small basement winery.

His dedication to the art and his years of experience were rewarded as Guglielmo wines became well known, particularly within San Francisco's French and Italian communities.

After weathering the devastating effects of Prohibition, Emilio and his son, George, expanded and modernized the winery. The operation has since passed to George's sons, George Jr. and Gene.

Although expansions and stucco have given the complex of buildings a more contemporary appearance, the atmosphere and charm of the old days have been retained. The old homestead is still here, and the basement still functions as part of the winery. Additions to the post-Repeal ivy-covered storage building have, at least in style, been consistent with the old structures. At the center of the grounds, a refurbished bunkhouse, sporting a new Tudor facade, serves as tasting room and offices.

In addition to its roster of more than a dozen varietals, Guglielmo bottles a line of premium table and specialty wines under the name Emile's. These include champagne, sherry, vermouth, fruit wines, and brandy.

Estate Bottled
1982
FUMANTE
SANTA CLARA VALLEY DRY WHITE WINE

Produced and Bottled by Emilio Guglielmo Winery,
Morgan Hill, Santa Clara Valley, California
BW 3656 Alcohol 12% by Volume.

1480 East Main Avenue
Morgan Hill, CA 95037
(408) 779-2145

HOURS: 9 A.M.–5 P.M. daily
TASTINGS: Yes
TOURS: By appointment
PICNIC AREA: Yes
RETAIL SALES: Yes
DIRECTIONS: One-and-a-half miles from downtown Morgan Hill on East Main.

Sycamore Creek Vineyards

Morgan Hill

In contrast to their neighbor, Nikola Kirigin-Chargin of Kirigin Cellars, who has been making wine for most of his life, Terry and Mary Kaye Parks are the new kids on the block.

Former schoolteachers, the Parks joined the "back-to-the-land" movement and bought an aging ranch in the Uvas Valley. After spending a few years fixing the place and dabbling in home winemaking, they learned that the nearby Marchetti Winery was for sale and went to take a look. "Terry fell in love with the place," recalled Mary Kaye.

The vines at Sycamore Creek are a mix of old and new. About half of the sixteen acres is comprised of vines that date back to the early 1900s.

The resulting wines—Zinfandel and Cabernet Sauvignon—have consistently won top honors in state competitions. The Parks also purchase grapes from neighboring vineyards and from other California vineyards.

Sycamore Creek's many awards are displayed prominently behind the bar in the rustic tasting room, a converted hayloft inside the old winery barn. Large windows have been installed in the tasting loft to provide sweeping views of the creek, the vineyards, and the mountains beyond.

Because of the size of their operation—the annual capacity is between 4,000 and 5,000 cases—the Parks are able to give their wines a personal attention not possible at larger wineries. They are particularly proud of the fact that Sycamore Creek white wines are chemical free—fermented without the addition of SO_2.

The winery at Sycamore Creek is a family operation. Visitors are likely to find Terry and Mary Kaye behind the bar and at the controls of the bottling equipment. Even their two young sons pitch in.

While picnic facilities are not available at Sycamore Creek, Santa Clara County maintains a small picnic and rest area just a few miles away on Watsonville Road between the winery and Highway 152.

12775 Uvas Road
Morgan Hill, CA 95037
(408) 779-4738

HOURS: Noon–5 P.M. Saturday and Sunday
TASTINGS: Yes
TOURS: By appointment
PICNIC AREA: No
RETAIL SALES: Yes
DIRECTIONS: From Hecker Pass Road (Highway 152), north on Watsonville Road to Uvas Road intersection.
VINTNER'S CHOICE: Zinfandel and Cabernet Sauvignon

Kirigin Cellars

Gilroy

The communist takeover of Croatia (now Yugoslavia) in 1945 spelled the end of the generations-old winemaking operation of the Kirigin-Chargin family. After the new goverment took over the winery, vintner Nikola Kirigin-Chargin decided to take his family and leave their homeland. "I could live without wine, but not without freedom," he said.

The family emigrated in 1959, and Kirigin-Chargin resumed his career in the United States, serving as winemaker at San Martin and Almaden Wineries.

Kirigin-Chargin, who holds a degree in enology from the University of Zagreb, called upon his education and years of European and American winemaking experience in striking out on his own in the Uvas Valley of Santa Clara County.

Housed in the old Bonesio Winery, which was established in 1833, Kirigin Cellars (pronounced Kuh-REE-gun) has, since 1976, successfully combined old world and modern winemaking technologies.

The equipment used by the winery is among the most modern to be found in this region, according to the winemaker. New 3,000-gallon stainless steel tanks hold the fermenting juices, while the clearing, maturing, and aging processes occur in redwood tanks and small oak barrels in Kirigin-Chargin's insulated cellar. The vats are contained in an old wooden barn which in more recent years has been covered with tan-colored stucco.

In addition to the more than one dozen red and white varietals, Kirigin Cellars markets dessert wines, including a Vine de Mocca, which carries a rich coffee flavor.

Visitors to Kirigin Cellars enter the unassuming, dimly lit tasting room through a door fashioned from a weathered wine barrel. The room sits behind the family residence, a grand old home once owned by millionaire Henry Miller, a turn-of-the-century cattle baron. While the Millers lived in high style, Kirigin-Chargin and his wife enjoy a simpler existence. "I bought this winery for pleasure," he said. "At my age, to think I'll become rich is foolish."

Kirigin Cellars

California
Gewurztraminer
VINTAGE 1979

*Produced from 100% Gewurztraminer Grapes:
Arroyo Seco Vyds., Monterey*

PRODUCED AND BOTTLED BY KIRIGIN CELLARS
Gilroy, Santa Clara Co., California • Alcohol 12% by Vol.

11550 Watsonville Road
Gilroy, CA 95020
(408) 847-8827

HOURS: 9 A.M.–6 P.M. daily
TASTINGS: Yes
TOURS: By appointment
PICNIC AREA: Yes
RETAIL SALES: Yes
DIRECTIONS: From Hecker Pass Road (Highway 152), north on Watsonville Road.
VINTNER'S CHOICE: Kirigin-Chargin doesn't enter wine competitions and refuses to acknowledge a favorite. "I like all my wines," he says.

Sarah's Vineyard

Gilroy

A honking gaggle of geese sounded my arrival at Sarah's Vineyard, a tiny Hecker Pass winemaking operation bonded in 1978. The name is a figment of the imagination of winemaker Marilyn Otteman who, with husband, John, owns and operates the establishment which, despite its young age, is earning a statewide reputation for its Chardonnay.

"A winery must have at least two personnel," John told me. "A winemaker and a hose dragger. I'm the hose dragger." The couple met some years ago while Marilyn was working at a home winemaking store in southern California. Together, they built Sarah's, an immaculate little redwood-sided winery that sits on the side of a hill just under the Otteman home.

Visitors park at the end of a long driveway off Highway 152 and walk a few hundred yards through Chardonnay vineyards to the winery—along with an escort of geese, who share the property with assorted other animals.

The vineyard at Sarah's consists of seven acres, all Chardonnay, planted in 1980 by friends whose names are immortalized on a sign posted among the vines. The first harvest was in 1983. Using grapes purchased from other vineyards, the winery also bottles Zinfandel, Cabernet, and Johannisberg Riesling.

"Most everything is hand done," explained John, as he and a friend lovingly applied labels to and polished a case of bottles. Although the Ottemans anticipate an expanded warehouse and a new storage cellar, they plan to keep the winery small.

In addition to their prize-winning Chardonnay, the Ottemans are proud of their distinctive label, the detail work for which was drawn by an engraver from Smith and Wesson, the arms manufacturer. (John is a collector of antique small arms.)

Sarah's, which once opened its gates on weekends for public tastings without appointment, now offers tours and tastings on a call-ahead basis, the result of growing demand for the Ottemans' wines. According to John, "Our wine is virtually all spoken for."

Sarah's Vineyard

1982
Monterey County
Chardonnay
Ventana Vineyard

Produced and Bottled by Sarah's Vineyard B.W. 4868
Gilroy, California • Alcohol 12.7% by volume

4005 Hecker Pass Highway
Gilroy, CA 95020
(408) 842-4278

HOURS: By appointment
TASTINGS: By appointment
TOURS: By appointment
PICNIC AREA: No
RETAIL SALES: Yes
DIRECTIONS: East of Watsonville Road intersection on Highway 152.
VINTNER'S CHOICE: Chardonnay

Summerhill Vineyards

Gilroy

With its contemporary ranch-style tasting room, Summerhill Vineyards presents an image of a newer winery. First impressions can be deceiving, however; this venerable estate has been producing wine since the Bertero family founded the operation in 1917.

Although the Berteros no longer own the property, the winery is still a family business. The husband-wife team of Debra Dodd and Red Johnson left Carmel to operate Summerhill as a small corporation comprised of family friends.

Debra and Red prefer not to lead tours through the winemaking facilities, steering visitors instead to one of the more comfortable tasting rooms in the area. In addition to daily tastings, Summerhill offers outdoor Sunday brunches from May through October. The winery also hosts an end-of-harvest dinner which doubles as a Halloween costume party. Details of the special events are included in Summerhill's newsletter.

Among Summerhill's lengthy roster of varietals and generics are several fruit wines and an Italian afterdinner wine called Aleatico, which is produced at only one other California winery.

CLASSIC CALIFORNIA

RIESLING

light in style and fruity, almost dry. Excellent with salad, seafood, or as a social wine. Serve slightly chilled.

CELLARED AND BOTTLED IN THE SHADOWS OF STEINBECK'S BELOVED COASTAL GAVILAN MOUNTAINS BY

SUMMERHILL VINEYARDS

Bonded Winery CA 1625 • Carmel, California • Alcohol 12% by Volume

3920 Hecker Pass Highway
Gilroy, CA 95020
(408) 842-3032

HOURS: 9 A.M.–6 P.M. daily
TASTINGS: Yes
TOURS: No
PICNIC AREA: Yes
RETAIL SALES: Yes
DIRECTIONS: Four miles west of Highway 101 in Gilroy on Hecker Pass Road.
VINTNER'S CHOICE: Santa Clara County, vintner-grown Cabernet Sauvignon Blanc (1983)

Live Oaks Winery

Gilroy

After a full day spent with several vintners of the Hecker Pass area, I hesitated before driving down the lane to Peter Scagliotti's Live Oaks Winery. From the road, the nondescript group of old buildings didn't appear to offer anything that I hadn't already seen.

My preconceptions were shattered when I stepped into what has to be one of Northern California's most eccentric tasting rooms. While Peter is a collector, he's not your typical collector. The large room is crammed with groupings of unconventional bric-a-brac. On one wall hang hundreds of business cards and vehicle license plates. Animal trophies are mounted on another. Behind the bar is an assemblage of foreign currency, while Christmas ornaments dangle (this was in May) from the ceiling.

The other buildings at Live Oaks Winery aren't open to the public, but most visitors seem content to browse among the curios that fill the tasting room. Peter does, however, maintain a comfortable picnic area and barbeque just outside the tasting room door.

Live Oaks, which was founded in 1912 by Peter's Italian immigrant father, Eduardo, is known for its premium-quality Burgundy. This blend of vintages and varieties is aged for more than five years before release.

3875 Hecker Pass Highway
Gilroy, CA 95020
(408) 842-2401

HOURS: 8 A.M.–5 P.M. daily; closed major
   holidays
TASTINGS: Yes
TOURS: No
PICNIC AREA: Yes
RETAIL SALES: Yes
DIRECTIONS: Four-and-a-half miles
   from downtown Gilroy on Hecker Pass
   Highway.
VINTNER'S CHOICE: Burgundy

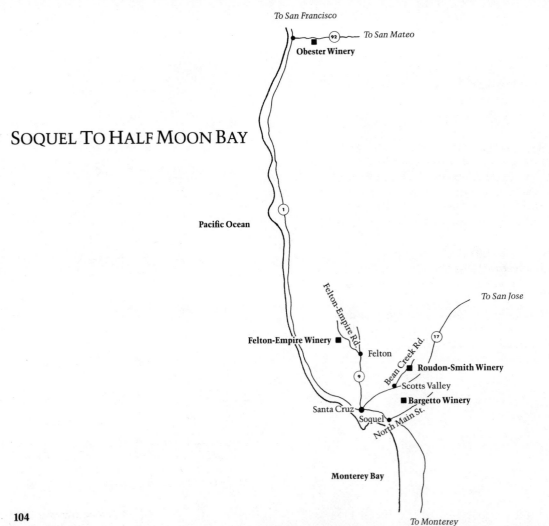

SOQUEL TO HALF MOON BAY

To San Francisco

(92) *To San Mateo*

Obester Winery

Pacific Ocean

(1)

Felton-Empire Rd.

Felton-Empire Winery

Felton

To San Jose

(17)

Bean Creek Rd.

Roudon-Smith Winery

(9)

Scotts Valley

Bargetto Winery

Santa Cruz

Soquel

North Main St.

Monterey Bay

To Monterey

Bargetto Winery

Soquel

At Bargetto Winery in Soquel, winemaking is not *just* a family affair, it's almost exclusively a family affair. Beverly, Martin, John, Richard, Loretta, Donna, Peter, James, and Tom all share the family name; each lends his or her own special talent to the operation.

Bargetto has been a fixture of this Santa Cruz County hamlet since 1933, the year Prohibition ended. John and Philip Bargetto, sons of an Italian winemaker who emigrated in the late 1800s, chose the year of Repeal to convert their truck farm to a small winery. They began, inauspiciously enough, making bulk wines for local retailers and restaurants.

John's son Lawrence guided the operation into its second generation and introduced fruit wines to the Bargetto roster. The apricot, pomegranate, raspberry, and olallieberry wines are still some of Bargettos' most popular.

After Lawrence's death in 1982, his widow, Beverly, assumed the presidency of the company. Son Martin serves as general manager, with a cadre of dedicated siblings and cousins rounding out the list of Bargetto staff.

Using grapes from other California vintners, the Bargetto family produces a number of varietals, including Johannisberg Riesling, Gewurztraminer, Chardonnay, Zinfandel, White Zinfandel, and Cabernet Sauvignon. The winery, housed in a tidy brown barn, also offers patrons a Blanc de Noir Methode Champenoise and a series of dessert wines imported from Italy.

In comfort and ambience, the Bargetto tasting room has few rivals. The narrow room with full length bar and rustic paneling perches at the edge of Soquel Creek. The homey environment indoors coupled with the peaceful setting beyond the windows lend themselves to lingering visits. Tastings are conducted under blue skies in an adjacent garden courtyard.

3535 North Main Street
Soquel, CA 95073
(408) 475-2258

HOURS: 10 A.M.–5:30 P.M. daily; except major holidays
TASTINGS: Yes
TOURS: 11 A.M. and 2 P.M. weekdays, by appointment
PICNIC AREA: No
RETAIL SALES: Yes
DIRECTIONS: From Highway 1, take Capitola-Soquel exit north to Main Street, turn right to winery 1 mile.
VINTNER'S CHOICE: Chardonnay

Roudon-Smith Vineyards

Scotts Valley

It had the makings of a contemporary Northern California success story: the engineering whiz who starts a promising manufacturing operation in high-tech Silicon Valley and gains fame and fortune. Jim Smith's story had most of the ingredients until fate stepped in and he hired Bob Roudon (Roo-DON) to help get the operation going. Bob, as it turned out, had different plans for himself and his new colleague, and it wasn't long before Jim was convinced to leave the Santa Clara Valley rat race and establish a vineyard and winery in the Santa Cruz foothills.

The Roudon and Smith families launched their partnership in 1971 with the planting of a small Chardonnay vineyard and the purchase of eighteen tons of grapes. The basement of Bob and Annamaria Roudon's Santa Cruz Mountains home served as the original winery until Jim and June Smith moved to a rural plot of land on Bean Creek Road and plans were drawn for a new winemaking facility. The two former engineers built much of the modest, fir-sided building themselves and even designed a few one-of-a-kind pieces of equipment for the winery.

In its relatively young life, Roudon-Smith has won praise from major wine critics and amassed a stable of prestigious California wine awards. Contributing to the efforts are Annamaria, who handles the finances and designs the labels, and June, who does the winery's public relations and marketing work.

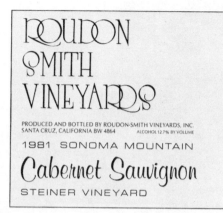

2364 Bean Creek Road
Santa Cruz, CA 95066
(408) 438-1244

HOURS: Saturdays, by appointment
TASTINGS: Saturdays, by appointment
TOURS: Saturdays, by appointment
PICNIC AREA: Yes
RETAIL SALES: Yes
DIRECTIONS: Call for appointment and directions.
VINTNER'S CHOICE: Zinfandel

Felton-Empire Vineyards

Felton

In establishing Hallcrest Vineyards in the early 1940s, San Francisco lawyer Chaffe Hall set out to produce European-quality wines on his own Santa Cruz Mountains estate. Striving for excellence in a region not known for fine wines, the maverick vintner spared no expense or effort, planting vines imported from Europe and enlisting help from a University of California professor.

True to his word, Hall turned his burgeoning winery into a leader. Although it garnered awards at the California State Fair for more than a decade, Hallcrest enjoyed only fleeting fame. Hall died in 1964 and the winery closed for twelve years.

While the Hallcrest name still appears on bottles of its estate-bottled wines, the establishment has, since 1976, been operated by a small corporation under the name of Felton-Empire Vineyards. Producing between 20,000 and 30,000 cases per year, Felton-Empire is today regaining the reputation that Chaffe Hall worked for in the early years. Ribbons from wine competitions adorn one wall in the tasting area of the winery.

Just over a dozen acres on the estate are planted to grapes. Purchases from other vineyards make possible a Maritime series of wines, blended from the juice of coast-grown berries.

The winery has more recently gained national fame for a line of nonalcoholic varietal juices. To produce some 15,000 cases of juice each year, Felton-Empire winemakers proceed as with wine, but bypass fermentation.

Single vineyard wines bottled here include White Riesling, Gewurztraminer, Chardonnay, Pinot Noir, Zinfandel, and Cabernet Sauvignon.

379 Felton-Empire Road
Felton, CA 95018
(408) 335-3939

HOURS: 11 A.M.–3 P.M. Saturday and Sunday
TASTINGS: Yes
TOURS: Informal, or guided
    by appointment
PICNIC AREA: Yes
RETAIL SALES: Yes
DIRECTIONS: One-quarter mile from town
    on Felton-Empire Road.
VINTNER'S CHOICE: White Riesling

Obester Winery

Half Moon Bay

The late John Gemello, who figured prominently in the post-Repeal rebirth of the South Bay Area wine industry with his own winery, left a legacy over the mountains in Half Moon Bay where a young couple is quietly carrying on a tradition begun in Italy nearly a century ago.

"It's strange the way things turn out," said Gemello's granddaughter, Sandy, recalling the events that led her and her husband, Paul Obester, to establish their small winery near the Pacific Ocean.

Several years after retiring from his winemaking business in Mountain View, the elder Gemello went to live with Sandy and Paul. In an attempt to provide her ninety-three-year-old grandfather with a project to occupy his time, Sandy suggested that he teach the family how to make wine. "One thing led to another," said Sandy, and the hobby evolved into a vocation when Paul, a Stanford University-educated Silicon Valley marketing executive, left his job to pursue a second career as winemaker. The Obesters bought some land on the outskirts of Half Moon Bay and established the winery in 1977.

Before John Gemello's death five years later at the age of ninety eight, the master winemaker touched another, even younger generation. Paul and Sandy's oldest son Doug studied at the University of California, Davis, and plans to follow in his great-grandfather's footsteps.

In addition to their responsibilities at Obester, Paul and Sandy commute regularly to Mountain View to oversee the operation of Gemello Winery, which they acquired a few years ago. Paul is president of Gemello and co-winemaker at Obester. Sandy is the winemaker at the Mountain View site and assists her husband at their own winery.

Obester (the accent is on the *O*) sits in a small valley beside the country highway that connects Half Moon Bay with San Mateo. An aging tin-sided hay barn functions as the production facility. Visitors are welcomed at a spacious and rustic tasting room that the Obesters fashioned from a carport. A picture window frames a scenic view of the valley.

12341 San Mateo Road (Highway 92)
Half Moon Bay, CA 94019
(415) 726-9463

HOURS: 10 A.M.–5 P.M. Friday through Sunday
TASTINGS: Yes
TOURS: By appointment
PICNIC AREA: Yes
RETAIL SALES: Yes
DIRECTIONS: From Highway 1, 2 miles east on Highway 92.
VINTNER'S CHOICE: Johannisberg Riesling

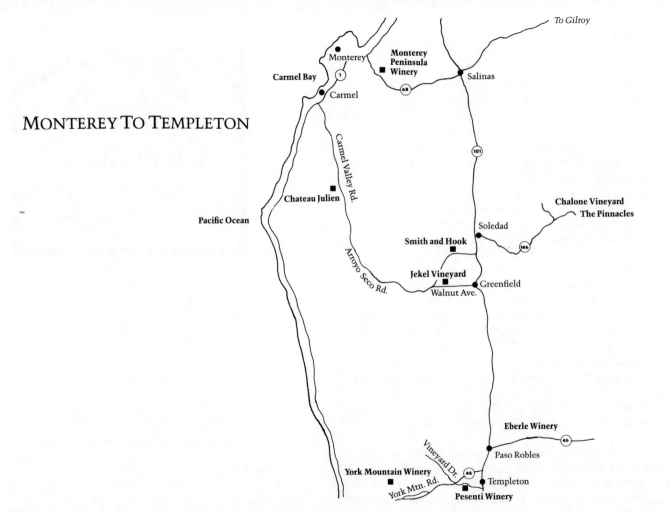

MONTEREY TO TEMPLETON

Pacific Ocean

Carmel Bay

Monterey

Carmel

Monterey Peninsula Winery

Salinas

To Gilroy

Carmel Valley Rd.

Chateau Julien

Arroyo Seco Rd.

Smith and Hook

Jekel Vineyard

Walnut Ave.

Greenfield

Soledad

Chalone Vineyard
The Pinnacles

Eberle Winery

Paso Robles

Vineyard Dr.

York Mountain Winery

York Mtn. Rd.

Pesenti Winery

Templeton

114

Monterey Peninsula Winery

Monterey

A stone-walled former ranch house built in the 1920s is enjoying a new life as the home of Monterey Peninsula Winery, which in 1984 celebrated its first decade of production.

Once part of a Spanish land grant known as Rancho Saucito, the property now sits at the end of the Monterey airport runway outside of town. The winery is the pride and joy of Roy Thomas and Deryck Nuckton, the two local dentists who chose the hacienda-type structure to reflect their old world approach to winemaking.

Their wines—only 10,000 cases are produced each year—are tended by hand, fermented in small batches, and clarified in their casks. In giving special attention to the varying character of the grapes culled from vineyards throughout the state, it's not unusual for the winemakers to produce more than a dozen lots of Zinfandel from a single vintage. (Monterey Peninsula has developed a reputation for its full-bodied reds.)

The aging wines are provided with a near perfect home in the cave-like environment created by the building's five-and-a-half-foot-thick limestone walls. Rows of barrels are stacked nearly to the cobweb-laden rafters in the rustic tasting area. Visitors stand at a long bar, at one end of which are displayed the winery's several awards.

Monterey Peninsula bottles numerous wines, including a Black Burgundy and a selection of dessert varieties. As many as twenty may be available for tasting on a given day.

Monterey Peninsula Winery 1979 San Luis Obispo Zinfandel Wilpete Farms, Willow Creek
PRODUCED AND BOTTLED BY MONTEREY PENINSULA WINERY MONTEREY, CALIFORNIA ALCOHOL 13.9% BY VOLUME

2999 Monterey-Salinas Highway
Monterey, CA 93940
(408) 372-4949

HOURS: 10 A.M.–sunset, daily
TASTINGS: Yes
TOURS: By appointment
PICNIC AREA: Yes
RETAIL SALES: Yes
DIRECTIONS: Two miles from Highway 1 on Monterey-Salinas Highway.
VINTNER'S CHOICE: Zinfandel

Chateau Julien

Carmel

The corporate offices of an east coast oil company are a long way, both physically and figuratively, from a wine estate on the California coast. Nonetheless, petroleum company executive Bob Brower and his wife, Pat, were happy to trade their existence in New York for life in peaceful Carmel Valley.

As the winery's name and appearance suggest, the Browers were inspired by the fine country wineries of France. Wines are produced in the French claret tradition of Bordeaux, using state-of-the-art equipment and imported bottles. The French oak cooperage is exchanged for new barrels after each vintage.

Chateau Julien has only a small experimental vineyard on site and consequently purchases grapes from growers elsewhere in Monterey County and from the Paso Robles region farther south. The roster here includes Chardonnay, Sauvignon Blanc, Fume Blanc, Merlot, and Cabernet Sauvignon. Chateau Julien also produces a Julien Dry Sherry, Carmel Cream Sherry, and two table wines.

The chateau itself, which was to be expanded for additional storage, is a grand two-story building of white plaster, built in 1983, one year after the first vintage. In addition to the Great Hall reception and tasting area with its tiled floor and large stained glass windows, the building contains offices and an elegant conference room for private functions. Barrels are stored adjacent to the fermentation tanks at the opposite end of the facility, while production equipment is set on a pad outside.

Local ordinances discourage drop-in visits for tours and tastings. "Invitations" are available by calling in advance of a weekend visit.

8940 Carmel Valley Road
Carmel, CA 93923
(408) 624-2600

HOURS: 10 A.M.–5 P.M. Saturday; Noon–5 P.M.
Sunday; weekdays by appointment
TASTINGS: By appointment
TOURS: By appointment
PICNIC AREA: No
RETAIL SALES: Yes
DIRECTIONS: Five miles east of Highway 1 on Carmel Valley Road.
VINTNER'S CHOICE: Chardonnay

Smith and Hook

Gonzales

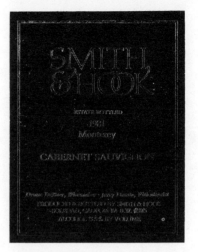

"A commitment to Cabernet" is the slogan of Smith and Hook, a wine estate whose sole product is—you guessed it. Some 250 rolling acres on the eastern slope of the Santa Lucia Mountains provide the panoramic setting for this interesting looking winery.

The operation is housed in an old barn whose former occupants were quarter horses. The stable sits on the old Smith Ranch while the adjacent Hook property is planted to grapes—hence the winery's name.

The site, which affords breathtaking views of the Salinas Valley and Gavilan Mountains, was chosen in 1973 by the McFarland Wine Company of Southern California. The McFarlands, longtime wine grape growers, concentrated their planting efforts on Cabernet vines and celebrated their first harvest in 1979.

The family may have drastically altered the function of the old horse ranch, but they preserved the property's rustic look. The stable was reconditioned to house winemaking equipment, open redwood fermentors, and rows of barrels. The old tack room is now the laboratory, and what was a bunkhouse now serves as an office. Guests are welcomed at another original building that overlooks the valley. The only new facility is a warehouse built to accommodate small oak cooperage.

Winemaker Duane DeBoer oversees the operation and is responsible for ensuring the quality of Smith and Hook Cabernet. Grapes from the several varying slopes and valleys of the vineyard are hand picked and crushed in separate batches. After one year of aging, the wines are blended (along with some Merlot) to obtain the desired quality. Smith and Hook wines are aged for three years—or even longer, if the winemaker so chooses.

37700 Foothill Road
P.O. Box 1010
Gonzales, CA 93926
(408) 675-2311 or 678-2132

HOURS: By appointment
TASTINGS: By appointment
TOURS: By appointment
PICNIC AREA: Yes
RETAIL SALES: No
DIRECTIONS: From Highway 101, west on Arroyo Seco Road, right on Fort Romie, left on Colony, right on Foothill, and left on driveway at school.
VINTNER'S CHOICE: Cabernet Sauvignon (their only wine)

Chalone Vineyard

Soledad

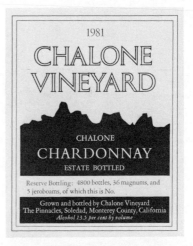

Chalone Vineyard takes its name from an extinct volcano that shaped the Gavilan Range centuries ago. The region's grape-growing potential was tapped in the early 1900s by a Frenchman who discovered conditions that compared favorably with the famous Cote d'Or of his homeland. Vines planted during the 1920s and 1940s first produced grapes that were sent away and used in making Soledad Champagne.

Since then the property has seen a succession of proprietors. Earlier owners constructed a tidy little winery, which now holds Chalone's library of older vintages. Today, the little oak-shaded, whitewashed building is dwarfed by a modern winery which has a provision for even further expansion should production warrant.

Chalone, which started out in the mid-sixties as a small partnership, is now a publicly held company—a rarity nowadays in the California wine-making industry. Chairman of the board Richard Graff, vineyard manager Bob Roche, and winemaker Michael Michaud supervise the hand picking of berries in small lots, with each acre yielding only about three to five barrels of wine.

While many of Chalone's 120 acres of vineyard are relatively new, the original vines still produce. In fact, the reserve wines from these craggy old vines are available only to those who write for an appointment and make the half-hour trek from the valley floor up to this oldest winery in Monterey County.

Stonewall Canyon Road
P.O. Box 855
Soledad, CA 93960
(415) 441-8975

HOURS: By appointment (please write for
   appointment)
TASTINGS: By appointment
TOURS: By appointment
PICNIC AREA: No
RETAIL SALES: Yes
DIRECTIONS: From Soledad, 9 miles east on
   Highway 146; 1 mile on Stonewall
   Canyon Road to winery.
VINTNER'S CHOICE: Chardonnay and Pinot
   Noir

Jekel Vineyard

Greenfield

From a distance, Jekel Vineyard more closely resembles a rambling country estate. In addition to a weathered old barn, there's a windmill and a new red, two-story addition which from the road looks like a fine old ranch house.

A winery it is, however, albeit a new one. The Jekel family established their vineyard on the outskirts of Greenfield in 1974, converting row crops to vines. The winery followed four years later. When I visited Jekel, more than 300 acres were under cultivation, providing the winery with enough grapes to produce 50,000 cases per year.

Production is centered in a large galvanized barn painted red. Towering stainless steel fermentors, a laboratory, barrel storage, and a bottling room are within a few steps of each other. While a tour of Jekel's facilities is worthwhile, visitors can also view some of the operation from interior windows in the intimate tasting room.

With the completion of the new wing, the Jekel family transferred the business headquarters from their home base in Southern California to the winery. Along with the offices, the addition houses a hospitality area that accommodates group luncheons and tastings.

The lengthy and cool growing season of the Arroyo Seco district enables Jekel to produce some award-winning wines, including Johannisberg Riesling, Chardonnay, Pinot Blanc, Pinot Noir, and Cabernet Sauvignon.

40155 Walnut Avenue
Greenfield, CA 93927
(408) 674-5522

HOURS: 10 A.M.–5 P.M. Thursday–Monday
TASTINGS: Yes
TOURS: By appointment
PICNIC AREA: Yes
RETAIL SALES: Yes
DIRECTIONS: One mile west of Highway 101 on Walnut Avenue.
VINTNER'S CHOICE: Johannisberg Riesling

Eberle Winery

Paso Robles

Eberle Winery had been open scarcely one week when I happened by in the spring of 1984. Gary and Jeanie Eberle were still at work applying the finishing touches to the sparkling, wood-sided facility which perches on a hill a few miles east of Paso Robles.

The rolling land surrounding the winery was bare when I visited, but the Eberles were preparing to plant forty acres of vines here. Until then, Gary planned to continue buying grapes elsewhere.

The Eberles' first priority was building the winery, and in doing so, the couple went first class. The tasting room is a large one, trimmed with oak and sporting a large, tiled fireplace. From one window, visitors can view the outdoor crushing pad; from another, the interior fermentation and storage areas can be seen. At the end of the bar, French doors open up to a covered patio that overlooks the expansive estate and the hills beyond.

Prior to establishing his own winery, Gary practiced the vintner's art at nearby Estrella Winery, which he designed and built. Also a wine industry veteran, Jeanie operates a wine wholesale business from the building.

Gary's 1980 Cabernet accompanied President Reagan on his 1984 trip to China. This vintage was part of the 75th anniversary memento wine collection of the University of California, Davis.

The Eberle roster is short at present, featuring only Cabernet Sauvignon, Chardonnay, and Muscat Canelli. The latter is sold only at the winery.

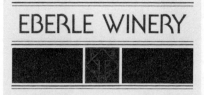

Highway 46
P.O. Box 2459
Paso Robles, CA 93447
(805) 238-9607

HOURS: 10 A.M.–5 P.M. daily; closed major holidays

TASTINGS: Yes

TOURS: Yes

PICNIC AREA: Yes

RETAIL SALES: Yes

DIRECTIONS: Four miles east of Highway 101 on Highway 46.

VINTNER'S CHOICE: Cabernet Sauvignon

Pesenti Winery

Templeton

For a relatively small, family-run business, Pesenti Winery offers an unusually lengthy stable of wines. The list of more than eighty different types is not a roster for the indecisive wine enthusiast.

Some of the wines are made from grapes that flourish among original vines planted by founder Frank Pesenti in 1923. A native of Bergamo, Italy, Frank had to wait until Prohibition ended to establish his winery. The original, built in 1934, has since been enlarged twice as the business grew.

The facility consists of two large, plain buildings painted white. One contains concrete fermentation tanks, crushing equipment, and the tasting room, where the array of Pesenti wines covers almost every inch of wall space. Aging and bottling take place in the adjacent masonry building. The family homestead stands nearby.

Frank's son, Vic; Vic's brother-in-law, Al Nerelli; and Al's son, Frank, share the operation of the winery these days. While poking around the place, I asked a winery employee for the name of Pesenti's winemaker. "We all help make wine," he joked. "Everybody gets to work their feet."

2900 Vineyard Drive
Templeton, CA 93465
(805) 434-1030

HOURS: 8 A.M.–5:30 P.M. Monday–Saturday; 9 A.M.–5:30 P.M. Sunday
TASTINGS: Yes
TOURS: Informal
PICNIC AREA: No
RETAIL SALES: Yes
DIRECTIONS: From Highway 101 south of Paso Robles, take Vineyard Drive exit west 2.5 miles to winery.
VINTNER'S CHOICE: Zinfandel

York Mountain Winery

Templeton

York Mountain Winery has written its share of Templeton District winemaking history. This venerable establishment celebrated its centennial in 1982, making it one of the Central Coast's oldest wineries.

The establishment was christened Ascension Winery by Andrew York, who grew grapes and made small amounts of wine here in the late 1800s. The winery remained in the York family until Max Goldman purchased it in 1970. Max's son Steve is the winemaker, daughter Suzanne works the tasting room, and wife Cindy makes jams and jellies and other gift items sold here.

The Goldmans' operation is as rustic as you'll find in these parts. The brick-walled, dimly lit tasting room has a wood floor, a rustic stone fireplace, and an assortment of antique bric-a-brac. Outside is a small deck with a bench facing the scenic hills and vines.

Although Max bought the property with plans to concentrate on champagne, other wines have crept onto the roster. York Mountain produces Vin Rosé, red and white wine, Dry Sherry, Zinfandel, Chardonnay, Merlot, Pinot Noir, Cabernet Sauvignon, and two types of champagne.

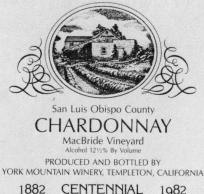

YORK MOUNTAIN

San Luis Obispo County
CHARDONNAY
MacBride Vineyard
Alcohol 12½% By Volume
PRODUCED AND BOTTLED BY
YORK MOUNTAIN WINERY, TEMPLETON, CALIFORNIA
1882   CENTENNIAL   1982

York Mountain Road
Route 2, Box 191
Templeton, CA 93465
(805) 238-3925

HOURS: 10 A.M.–5 P.M. daily
TASTINGS: Yes
TOURS: By appointment
PICNIC AREA: No
RETAIL SALES: Yes
DIRECTIONS: From Highway 101 south of Paso Robles, take Highway 46 west for 9 miles; north at first or second York Mountain Road sign.
VINTNER'S CHOICE: Zinfandel

THE MOTHER LODE AND CENTRAL VALLEY

There's Grapes in Them Thar Hills

California's Mother Lode is in the midst of a boom the likes of which hasn't been seen since James Marshall touched off the Gold Rush in 1848. Today's attraction is the grape.

A prominent wine-producing region during the last part of the nineteenth century and early part of the twentieth, the Sierra foothills later lost hundreds of acres of vineyards to *phylloxera* and through neglect during the years of Prohibition.

The gold country is rapidly making up for lost time; I found new vineyards emerging on hillsides and in valleys from Nevada County to Calaveras County. Wineries have likewise been springing up in recent years—so fast, in fact, that it's difficult to maintain a current count. While winemaking operations are scattered about much of the countryside, the highest concentrations are to be found east of Highway 49 along the northern portion of Amador County near Plymouth, and in El Dorado County, between Fairplay and Apple Hill.

The scenic backroads and tranquil towns—not to mention friendly vintners—make it difficult to leave this region after just one day. Consequently, if you're planning an overnight stay, consider the Mother Lode's array of historic small hotels and inns. Among the quaint hostelries you'll discover along your tour are the Murphys Hotel in Murphys, the Hotel Leger in Mokelumne Hill, the Sutter Creek Inn in Sutter Creek, and the National Hotel in Nevada City.

During the harvest season, when tourist attention is heaped upon the Napa and Sonoma grape-growing regions, the backroads of the Mother Lode present a delightful and relatively uncrowded alternative for wine enthusiasts and California adventurers.

The Sierra Foothills Winery Association publishes a visitors guide (see the Grape Escapes section at the back of this book) that lists its member wineries as well as other helpful information for those planning a trip into the hills.

The industry may be undergoing a rebirth in the foothills, but winemaking has flourished for years in the San Joaquin Valley. Considering the vastness of this wine-producing region and its tremendous contribution of grapes to the state's wine industry, one would think tasting rooms would be plentiful. Actually, they are few and even farther between.

I found myself attracted to the dwindling number of informal family-operated wineries that have been longtime valley fixtures. A visit with the Nonini family at their Fresno winery, for example, was among the highlights of my travels through Northern California's wine country. Winemaker Reno Nonini greets his guests at a tiny, unpretentious room where they sip valley vintages, not in crystal glasses but from paper cups pulled from a wall dispenser. This is backroad wining at its best.

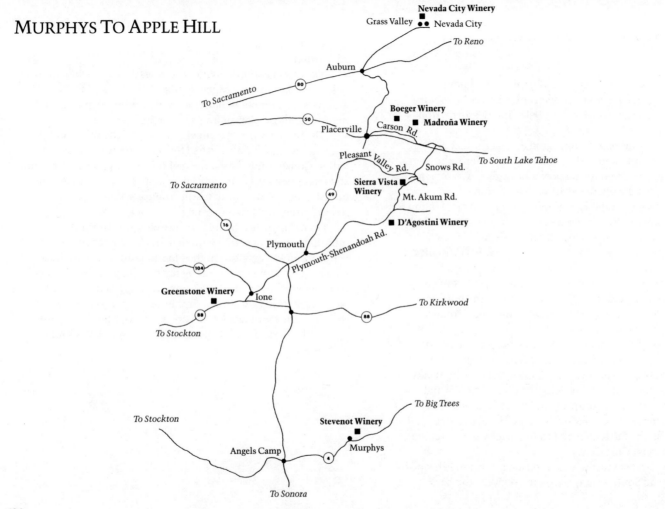

MURPHYS TO APPLE HILL

Nevada City Winery

Grass Valley ●● Nevada City

To Reno

Auburn

To Sacramento ⑧⑩

Boeger Winery

⑤⓪ ■ **Madroña Winery**

Placerville Carson Rd.

To South Lake Tahoe

Pleasant Valley Rd. Snows Rd.

Sierra Vista Winery ■

To Sacramento

④⑨ Mt. Akum Rd.

①⑥ ■ **D'Agostini Winery**

Plymouth

Plymouth-Shenandoah Rd.

⑩④

Greenstone Winery ■ Ione

⑧⑧ ⑧⑧ *To Kirkwood*

To Stockton

To Big Trees

To Stockton **Stevenot Winery** ■

Angels Camp ④ Murphys

To Sonora

Stevenot Winery

Murphys

For many years Mercer Cavern provided the only reason for tourists to venture down Sheep Ranch Road out of the little town of Murphys. Since Barden Stevenot established a vineyard in the neighborhood in 1976, however, the cavern has learned to share the spotlight.

The winery that bears Stevenot's name sits a couple of miles from Murphys in a small canyon ringed by oak and pine. Old timers might remember the spread as the Shaw Ranch, site of Calaveras County's first swimming pool.

The homestead and pool are still here, but the cattle have been replaced by nearly thirty acres of young vines. The age of the winery notwithstanding, Stevenot (the second *t* is silent) boasts a lengthy list of regional and state awards, many for the popular Zinfandel Blanc. Stevenot also produces Chardonnay, Chenin Blanc, Cabernet Sauvignon, and a Zinfandel that is served at Yosemite's famed Ahwahnee Hotel.

A number of renovated ranch buildings comprise the operation. Stevenot, whose family has resided in the county for five generations, lives in the stately old home with his wife, Debbie, proprietor of Harvest Cellars in Placerville. A barn that dates back to the 1890s houses the winemaking equipment. When things occasionally go awry here, workers blame the ghost of an Indian who, according to legend, was hanged in the barn long ago.

Of similar vintage is Stevenot's one-of-a-kind tasting room. Alaska House, as it is known, is an old log-walled, sod-roofed cellar of sorts, cut into a gentle grassy slope near the house. Rancher Shaw, who settled the property, chose this architectural style after returning from journeys to the Alaskan wilderness, where such earth-covered structures were common. At one time, this rustic bower, built in 1908, was home to a convicted murderer whom Shaw befriended.

But like the proverbial wine that mellows with age, the wild activities that colored the early years of the ranch have given way to a more respectable standing for Stevenot as one of the gold country's preeminent wineries.

We are a premium winery located in the historic gold rush country of the Sierra Foothills. Our Zinfandel - Blanc was produced from complementing Amador vineyards of different elevations. Capturing the intense fruitiness of the varietal results in the light salmon color.

Residual sugar 2% by weight. 6400 cases were bottled.

1982

Amador County

Zinfandel-Blanc

PRODUCED AND BOTTLED BY STEVENOT WINERY MURPHYS, CALAVERAS COUNTY, CALIFORNIA
B.W. 4839   ALCOHOL 11% BY VOLUME

2690 San Domingo Road
P.O. Box 548
Murphys, CA 95247
(209) 728-3436

HOURS: 10 A.M.–5 P.M. daily; closed major holidays
TASTINGS: Yes
TOURS: Weekdays only
PICNIC AREA: Yes
RETAIL SALES: Yes
DIRECTIONS: At Murphys Hotel, take Sheep Ranch Road/San Domingo Road for 2.5 miles; winery is 1 mile past Mercer Cavern.
VINTNER'S CHOICE: Cabernet Sauvignon

Greenstone Winery

Ione

A nationwide search for just the right spot brought two young Southern California families to the base of the Amador County foothills near Ione. Home winemakers Stan and Karen Van Spanje and Durward and Jane Fowler claimed the site in 1980 after touring the United States looking for a vineyard and winery location.

Situated a quarter of a mile off Highway 88, Greenstone started out as a part-time project for the couples, who divided their time between teaching jobs in Southern California and their vineyard in the Sierra foothills. Then, in 1983 Stan and Durward left the classroom to devote their full attention to the growing winemaking operation. Because Karen and Jane still teach in neighboring Ione, the winery observes a school schedule: open for visitors on weekends only during the academic year and Wednesday through Sunday during much of the summer.

The vines at Greenstone were planted in rich soil around rock outcroppings. For the winery, the owners chose a peaceful spot amongst gnarled oaks at the foot of the hills. Gables and a steep roof adorn the picturesque building, fashioned in the style of a French country barn.

The crusher and press are located outside, leaving the barn for storage. Stan even uses the ample air space inside by baking his sherry on a narrow catwalk high among the rafters.

In addition to its own twenty-plus acres of grapes, Greenstone uses grapes from other Amador County vineyards to produce some 8,500 cases of more than a half-dozen different wines. Topping the roster are a White Zinfandel and a California Colombard that sell as fast as the vintners can bottle them.

P.O. Box 1164
Ione, CA 95640
(209) 2744-2238

HOURS: 10 A.M.–4 P.M. Saturdays and Sundays; same hours Wednesday through Sunday in July and August
TASTINGS: Yes
TOURS: Yes, informal
PICNIC AREA: Yes
RETAIL SALES: Yes
DIRECTIONS: Highway 88 and Jackson Valley Road, southwest of Ione.
VINTNER'S CHOICE: California Colombard

D'Agostini Winery

Plymouth

The Shenandoah Valley east of Plymouth has in recent years become a home to nearly a dozen small winemaking operations. However, even the combination of their years of operation can't come close to matching the more than a century of winemaking at D'Agostini, patriarch of Mother Lode wineries.

A state historical landmark, D'Agostini was established by Adam Uhlinger, who began planting vines here as early as 1856, when the local population was given more to tearing up the hills than to cultivating them.

Enrico D'Agostini, an Italian immigrant, acquired the operation from Uhlinger's son in 1911, signaling the start of another two generations of family operation. Brothers Henry, Michele, Tulio, and Armenio inherited the winery when their father died in the mid-fifties.

With the siblings approaching retirement age and their children choosing other vocations, the D'Agostinis sold the winery in 1984.

The first stop for visitors is usually an informal tasting room, housed in a concrete block building nearest the road. The real treat, however, is a self-guided walk through the labyrinthine cellar of locally quarried stone. Here oval oak barrels, some as old as the winery itself, share space with 17,000 gallon casks that tower over visitors. The making of D'Agostini wines takes place in an adjacent covered area. The grand old homestead sits atop the cellar.

Despite the impression created by the hulking cellar casks, D'Agostini is a small winery by industry standards, with attention to quality receiving a higher priority than quantity.

Route 2, Box 19
Plymouth, CA 95669
(209) 245-6612

HOURS: 9 A.M.–4:30 P.M. daily; closed major holidays
TASTINGS: Yes
TOURS: Yes, informal
PICNIC AREA: No
RETAIL SALES: Yes
DIRECTIONS: Eight miles northeast of Plymouth on Shenandoah Road.
VINTNER'S CHOICE: Zinfandel

Sierra Vista Winery

Placerville

The decision to establish a vineyard in the Sierra foothills signaled a radical change for John MacCready and his family. In leaving their native Ohio in 1973, John traded a comfortable career in electrical engineering, in which he holds a Ph.D., for the relatively insecure life of a farmer.

The family chose to sink new roots near the sleepy hamlet of Pleasant Valley. John faced a formidable task in establishing his vineyard in 1977, laboring long and hard clearing trees and brush. He was rewarded not only with a healthy thirty-one-acre plot of vines but with a breathtaking Sierra view long obscured by trees. The native ponderosa pines removed in the process provided the wood for John's rustic winery, which sits near the family home.

John and his wife, Barbara, who have joined the legion of winemakers rediscovering the grape-growing potential of the Mother Lode, produce about 5,000 cases each year. They invite visitors to drop by the winery for a weekend taste of Sierra Vista's Cabernet Sauvignon, Fume Blanc, White and Red Zinfandel, and Chardonnay. Sierra Sirah from a small test plot is sold only at the winery.

Estate Bottled
1981 CABERNET SAUVIGNON
El Dorado
SIERRA VISTA
GROWN, PRODUCED & BOTTLED BY SIERRA VISTA WINERY, BW 4791
PLACERVILLE, CALIFORNIA • ALCOHOL 13.5% BY VOLUME

4560 Cabernet Way
Placerville, CA 95667
(916) 622-7221

HOURS: 11 A.M.–5 P.M. Saturday and
    Sunday; other times by appointment
TASTINGS: Yes
TOURS: Yes
PICNIC AREA: Yes
RETAIL SALES: Yes
DIRECTIONS: Take Newton Road exit from
    Highway 50 east of Placerville, south
    on Newton Road, left on
    Pleasant Valley Road, and right on
    Leisure Lane.
VINTNER'S CHOICE: Cabernet Sauvignon

Madroña Vineyards

Camino

With Sierra peaks rising beyond well-kept rows of grapevines, the setting of Madroña Vineyards must rank as one of the most dramatic among California wineries. In terms of elevation—3,000 feet—you won't find a loftier vineyard, at least not in the state.

Dick Bush is the owner of California's highest vineyard, the name of which was inspired by a handsome madrone tree that serves as a centerpiece among the vines. The former engineer and his wife, Leslie, a teacher, planted a 35-acre parcel between 1972 and 1974, but it wasn't until 1980 that ground was broken for the winery. Another four years elapsed before the rustic tasting room was finished.

The winery, a modern, nondescript facility, is situated among conifer and oak trees and is somewhat difficult to locate. Visitors must first pass through either an apple ranch or a Christmas tree farm in order to reach Madroña.

Notwithstanding its location off the beaten path, the winery bustles with activity. I waited in line as the winemaker cheerfully juggled Sunday customers, deliveries, and phone calls.

He does manage to find time to produce 7,000 cases of Madroña Chardonnay, White Riesling, Gewurztraminer, White and Red Zinfandel, Cabernet Sauvignon, and Merlot. Dick also serves a separate clientele through custom processing of wines for other operations.

Gatlin Road
P.O. Box 454
Camino, CA 95709
(916) 644-5948

HOURS: 10 A.M.–5 P.M. Saturday; 1 P.M.–5 P.M. Sunday
TASTINGS: By appointment
TOURS: By appointment
PICNIC AREA: Informal
RETAIL SALES: Yes
DIRECTIONS: From Highway 50 east of Placerville, west on Carson Road, north through High Hill Ranch (apples) to winery.
VINTNER'S CHOICE: Chardonnay and Cabernet Sauvignon

Boeger Winery

Placerville

I discovered Boeger Winery quite by accident several years ago during the fall Apple Hill Days celebration sponsored by local apple growers. Greg and Susan Boeger had only recently set up shop in a new concrete block facility on a hill overlooking the tiny, 1850s Lombardo Winery, now the Boeger tasting room.

The ensuing years have been good to Boeger Winery. Since 1973, its wine has been hailed by critics throughout the nation, won awards too numerous to mention, and has even been selected as a presidential gift for England's Queen Elizabeth.

On a recent return visit, I was delighted to find that success had not spoiled Boeger, which remains one of the gold country's most hospitable and intriguing wineries.

Although dwarfed by the main winery upslope, the tasting room is still Boeger's most prominent building. One of the state's earliest wineries, the diminutive stone and mortar cellar is maintained in a state of arrested decay.

Still visible here are the ceiling chutes through which the crushed grapes were once fed from what used to be the production area on the second floor. The old press is displayed along with other memorabilia assembled by the Boegers.

Boeger's annual production of 10,000 cases consists of Chenin Blanc, Chardonnay, Sauvignon Blanc, Zinfandel, Cabernet Sauvignon, and Merlot. The winery bottles blended wines under the popular labels Sierra Blanc, Hangtown Gold, and Hangtown Red. (Placerville was known as Hangtown during the Gold Rush.)

A 1980 Boeger Zinfandel, whose commemorative label bore the inscription "Elizabeth II, Majestic Release, California Zinfandel," was presented by President Reagan to Queen Elizabeth during the monarch's 1983 visit to California. The Boeger selection was part of a large gift of California wines judged by the White House as "fit for a queen."

1709 Carson Road
Placerville, CA 95667
(916) 622-8094

HOURS: 10 A.M.–5 P.M. Wednesday–Sunday
TASTINGS: Yes
TOURS: Informal
PICNIC AREA: Yes
RETAIL SALES: Yes
DIRECTIONS: From Highway 50 east of Placerville, take the Schnell School Road exit to Carson Road, east to winery drive.
VINTNER'S CHOICE: Merlot

Nevada City Winery

Nevada City

Nevada City's once thriving winemaking industry, which came to a sudden halt with Prohibition, seemed destined to become a lost art until a group of wine and grape-growing enthusiasts resurrected the Nevada City Winery in 1980. The 130 or so acres of grapes now under cultivation in Nevada County pale in comparison to the half-million vines that flourished in the region in the 1880s. Nevertheless, to the owners of the county's only bonded winery, it's a start.

In reestablishing the winery, which a century ago stood a couple of blocks away, the owners set up shop in a rustic garage that was part of an old foundry next door. (The historic foundry now houses the American Victorian Museum.)

Conversion of the garage to a small winery involved construction of a mezzanine above the production area. This perch serves as the tasting area and allows visitors to watch the nuts and bolts of winemaking while sampling the wares. The second floor is reserved for cooperage storage.

In addition to choosing an unusual facility, the operators of Nevada City Winery have adopted some uncommon techniques since the operation was revived a few years ago. Unlike some who buy grapes from varying regions, Nevada City winemaker Tony Norskog is highly selective. "We stress high-elevation grapes," said Norskog, who uses only those grapes grown above 2,000 feet. He said the 50 degree temperature variance from day to night at the loftier elevations "shuts the vines down overnight," creating the lively acidity that gives the wine a flavor all its own.

In keeping with the winery's unconventional image, Norskog has chosen not to rely exclusively on French and American oak barrels. Instead, he has been experimenting successfully with a practice that involves the introduction of planks fashioned from indigenous oak to stainless steel aging tanks, avoiding the bacteria problems, leakage, and evaporation sometimes associated with wooden cooperage. The reds, however, still spend some time in conventional barrels.

NEVADA CITY WINERY

Pinot Noir

1980

44 CASES PRODUCED   NEVADA COUNTY

Produced & Bottled by Nevada City Winery, Nevada City, California
Alcohol 11.8 Percent by Volume

321 Spring Street
Nevada City, CA 95959
(916) 265-WINE

HOURS: Noon–5 P.M. daily
TASTINGS: Yes
TOURS: Informal
PICNIC AREA: No
RETAIL SALES: Yes
DIRECTIONS: Downtown Nevada City.
VINTNER'S CHOICE: Douce Noir (1982)

FRESNO TO WINTERS

Winters
Winters Winery
Davis
Vacaville
R & J Cook Winery
Barengo–Lost Hills Vineyards
Acampo Rd.
Lodi
Stockton
Manteca
Escalon
Cadlolo Winery
Modesto
Merced
Madera
Shaw
Dickerson
Nonini Winery

A. Nonini Winery

Fresno

Don't let the urban sprawl of Fresno or the orchards along Highway 99 fool you. This is wine country. According to the Wine Institute, nearly half of California's annual wine grape crop is grown in the rich, warm district around Fresno.

The area is known primarily for the large wineries like Gallo which call this region home. However, several small operations are scattered along the back roads. Vineyards are everywhere. Even little Central High School has its own vineyard.

Among the grape growers who settled the valley in the early twentieth century was Antonio Nonini. An orphan who grew up in the Lombardia area at the base of the Italian Alps, Nonini left his homeland in 1900 at the age of twenty-one to seek a better life in the United States.

He bought several acres of Western Fresno County land and, with some gentle urging from his son, Reno, established the A. Nonini Winery in 1936.

Reno and his brothers, Geno and Gildo, took over the vineyards and winery after their father's death in 1959. Reno's son Thomas has also taken an active role as the winery enters its third generation of family operation.

Among Fresno County wineries, A. Nonini is the only one whose product is entirely grown by them. (The winery controls its own grapegrowing.) The Noninis produce table wines, most of which are sold locally. The premium vintages are aged in oak, the others in redwood tanks.

Tastings are conducted in a one-room cottage tucked between the Nonini homestead and the winery. A paper cup dispenser on the wall gives tasters an indication of the informality of the place. Although the winery is short on pomp, it's long on a hospitable atmosphere that has been a Nonini family tradition for nearly half a century.

2640 N. Dickenson Avenue
Fresno, CA 93711
(209) 275-1936

HOURS: 9 A.M.–6 P.M. Monday–Saturday
TASTINGS: Yes
TOURS: Yes
PICNIC AREA: No
RETAIL SALES: Yes
DIRECTIONS: From Highway 99 south, exit at McKinley; west 7 miles and .5 mile north on Dickenson. From the north, south on Highway 145 in Madera, east on Shaw, south on Dickenson.
VINTNER'S CHOICE: Zinfandel and Barbera

Cadlolo Winery

Escalon

In the San Joaquin Valley, where names like Gallo and Delicato are synonymous with winemaking, the comparatively tiny Cadlolo Winery has been forced to take a back seat. The winery, which is dwarfed by neighboring Franzia and ISC Wineries, is hidden away in the tiny town of Escalon.

Over the years the town has enveloped the historic winery, which is bordered on one side by a residential area and on the other by railroad tracks and the business section.

A Swiss vintner names Louis Sciaroni established the winery in 1913, erecting foot-thick brick walls to protect his wines from the blazing valley summer heat. The exterior is covered with a lime and sand mortar which today is painted a pleasing cream color.

Cadlolo was the name of Sciaroni's nephew, who purchased the winery in 1937. Cadlolo family members owned the business for several decades before selling the operation. Dorothy Murphy and her son, Bud Giles, are the newest owners.

Cadlolo appears quite small from the outside, but has a surprising capacity—nearly a quarter of a million gallons. Seventeen huge redwood tanks hold not only Cadlolo's ten varieties but a fair amount of wine made and stored here for other operations. The crusher and fermentation tanks sit outside next to the railroad tracks.

The only portion of the building not claimed for storage has been turned into a rustic tasting room filled with antiques.

CADLOLO OF CALIFORNIA
ESTABLISHED IN 1913

MELLOW RED WINE
ALCOHOL 12% BY VOLUME

BOTTLED BY
CADLOLO WINERY, ESCALON, CALIFORNIA

1124 California Street
Escalon, CA 95320
(209) 838-2457

HOURS: 10 A.M.–5 P.M. daily
TASTINGS: Yes
TOURS: By appointment
PICNIC AREA: Yes
RETAIL SALES: Yes
DIRECTIONS: From Highway 120 in Escalon, south on McHenry, right on California Street.
VINTNER'S CHOICE: Mellow Red

Barengo-Lost Hills Vineyards

Acampo

Spindly old palms line the stretch of road from Highway 99 to the tiny Central Valley burg of Acampo, home of Barengo–Lost Hills Vineyards. A valley fixture known for decades simply as Barengo Winery, the business was established in the 1930s by Camillo and Natale Barengo and Cesare Mondavi, father of well-known vintners Robert and Peter Mondavi. Camillo's son Dino later took over the winery.

After acquiring the venerable property in 1981, Bakersfield-based Verdugo Vineyards, Inc., began bottling under the Lost Hills label, a reference to an area in Kern County where Verdugo maintains a large vineyard.

In revitalizing a facility and equipment that were great with age, Verdugo spent nearly one million dollars, replacing old cooperage with stainless steel, adding a new filtration system, and installing a modern bottling line capable of processing a half-million cases each year.

These efforts have resulted in an impressive roster of wine products including several traditional varietals, German-style May and spiced wines, dessert wines, wine coolers, and wine vinegar.

While modern technology has caught up with the production areas, the winery has retained its vintage red brick façade. The only public area of Barengo–Lost Hills (tours have been discontinued) is the tasting room, which has also been relatively untouched. The room features a handsome copper-covered bar and a selection of deli and gift items. Part of an old 15,000 gallon redwood tank is visible through a large interior window.

Barengo–Lost Hills operates other tasting rooms in Santa Clara, Lodi (Highway 12 and Interstate 5), Red Bluff, and Torrance.

3125 E. Orange Street
Acampo, CA 95220
(209) 369-2746

HOURS: 9 A.M.–5 P.M. daily
TASTINGS: Yes
TOURS: No
PICNIC AREA: Yes
RETAIL SALES: Yes
DIRECTIONS: From Highway 99, exit at Acampo Road and drive 1 mile west to winery.
VINTNER'S CHOICE: Barengo Cremapri, Lost Hills White Zinfandel

R&J Cook

Clarksburg

If the label depicting an old sternwheeler suggests that R&J Cook is a bit unusual, a visit to the winery will confirm it. The husband-wife operation is one of very few wineries situated near the banks of the Sacramento River, which once carried riverboat travelers back and forth between the capital city and the Bay Area.

This region, although long-famous for its rich soil, has only recently gained any kind of notoriety for grape growing. It was the Cook family that put the Delta on the California winery maps.

The vineyards at Cook date from the late 1960s, when Perry Cook converted a small plot of his row crops to grapes. The quality of the resulting vintage led Perry and son Roger to plant additional vines. Planting expanded in the mid-1970s when Roger established another vineyard nearby in Solano County. Five years later, he and his wife, Joanne, launched their winery with help from their sons.

A tasting room is located next to the winery, which contains an assortment of modern winemaking equipment. The Cooks reside in an adjacent ranch house. The best views of R&J Cook are available from a river levee next to the vines, where Roger and Joanne have built a picnic area for their visitors.

Netherlands Road
P.O. Box 227
Clarksburg, CA 95612
(916) 775-1234

HOURS: 9 A.M.–4:30 P.M. weekdays;
    11 A.M.–4:00 P.M. weekends
TASTINGS: Yes
TOURS: By appointment
PICNIC AREA: Yes
RETAIL SALES: Yes
DIRECTIONS: Twelve miles south of
    Sacramento along the Sacramento
    River, take Netherlands Road 3 miles
    southwest of Clarksburg to the winery.
VINTNER'S CHOICE: Merlot Blanc

Winters Winery

Winters

Winters Winery is the latest occupant of a downtown Winters landmark which since 1876 has housed a general store, butcher shop, bakery, and a turn-of-the-century opera house and dining room.

In contrast to the previous tenants, winemaker David Storm was attracted by the building's thick brick walls and underground cellar, which he found to be well suited for winemaking.

Storm founded Winters Winery here in 1980 after working as a consulting civil and sanitary engineer. In addition to serving as a consultant to wineries on water and wastewater problems, he made wine at home for more than a decade before starting his commercial venture. The vintner earned bachelor's and master's degrees, as well as a doctorate, from nearby U.C., Davis.

Not only is the three-story building suitable for production and aging, it's an aesthetically pleasing site for a winery. Visitors are welcomed at a vintage, high-ceilinged room that has been attractively refitted for tastings and retail sales. Storm has furnished this public room with antique furniture and winemaking equipment. The street-level rooms also contain a laboratory and areas for fermentation and case storage. Aging takes place in the cellar.

The Winters Winery roster includes several varietals and two generics bottled as Putah Creek Red and Gold.

1981

Petite Sirah
California

WINTERS
WINERY

Naismith Vineyard, Madison, California

ALCOHOL 12.4% BY VOLUME
PRODUCED AND BOTTLED BY WINTERS WINERY   WINTERS, CALIFORNIA

15 Main Street
Winters, CA 95694
(916) 795-3201

HOURS: 10 A.M.–5 P.M. daily
TASTINGS: Yes
TOURS: By appointment
PICNIC AREA: No
RETAIL SALES: Yes
DIRECTIONS: Downtown Winters, .5 mile
   from Highway 128.
VINTNER'S CHOICE: Zinfandel

Grape Escapes

W hen planning a backroad winery tour, you may wish to schedule your trip to coincide with special wine-related events held regularly in many parts of the north state. Because schedules are subject to change, it is advisable to contact the sponsoring organization several weeks in advance of the dates noted.

Sonoma Valley
Russian River Wine Fest, Healdsburg, May. Call the Healdsburg Chamber of Commerce at (707) 433-6935.

Sonoma County Wine Auction, Geyserville, August. Call the Sonoma County Wine Growers group at (707) 527-7701.

Sonoma County Harvest Fair, Santa Rosa, September-October. Call the Sonoma County Visitors and Convention Bureau at (707) 545-1420.

Russian River Barrel Tastings, Russian River area wineries, first weekend in March. Call the Healdsburg Chamber of Commerce at (707) 433-6935.

Napa Valley
Napa Wine Festival and Crafts Fair, Napa, September. Call the Napa Chamber of Commerce at (707) 226-7455.

Napa Valley Wine Auction, St. Helena, Father's Day weekend. Call the Napa

Valley Vintners Association at (707) 963-0148.

Napa Valley Wine Symposium, Napa, February. Call the Napa Chamber of Commerce at (707) 226-7455.

The Central Coast
California Wine Festival, Monterey, Fall. Call the Monterey Peninsula Chamber of Commerce/Visitors and Convention Bureau at (408) 649-1770.

Festival of Monterey County Wine and Food, Monterey, Summer. Contact the Monterey Peninsula Chamber of Commerce/Visitors and Convention Bureau at (408) 649-1770.

Paso Robles Wine Festival, Paso Robles, third Saturday in May. Call the Paso Robles Chamber of Commerce at (805) 238-0506.

The Sierra
Sierra Showcase of Wine, Plymouth, May. Call the Amador County Chamber of Commerce at (209) 223-0350.

The Central Valley
The Lodi Grape Festival, Lodi, September. Call the Lodi Grape Festival at (209) 369-2771.

Wine Tour Maps

Maps that include updated regional listings of wineries along with hours and services are available from the following organizations:

The Russian River Wine Road (wineries and inns). Send $1 to the Russian River Wine Road, P.O. Box 127, Geyserville, CA 95441.

Wineries of Mendocino County. Send 50 cents to the Mendocino County Chamber of Commerce, P.O. Box 244, Ukiah, CA 95482.

Guide to Napa Valley Wineries. Send $1 to the Napa Chamber of Commerce, P.O. Box 636, Napa, CA 94559.

Guide to Wineries of the Redwood Empire (Napa, Sonoma, Marin, Lake and Mendocino counties). Write to Redwood Empire Association, One Market Plaza, Spear Street Tower #1001, San Francisco, CA 94105 (include 20 cents postage).

Winetrails of the Santa Cruz Mountains. Write to Santa Cruz Mountain Vintners Association, P.O. Box 2856, Saratoga, CA 95070.

Southern Santa Clara Valley Vintners Map. Write to P.O. Box 1062, Gilroy, CA 95021 (include 20 cents postage).

Wineries of Monterey County. Write to Monterey Peninsula Chamber of Commerce, P.O. Box 1770, Monterey, CA 93940.

Paso Robles Wine Festival Map. Write to Paso Robles Chamber of Commerce, P.O. Box 457, Paso Robles, CA 93447.

Winetasting in the Sierra Foothills (wineries, inns and restaurants). Write to Sierra Foothills Winery Association, P.O. Box 425, Somerset, CA 95684.

California's Wine Wonderland (complete listing of member wineries). Write to The Wine Institute, 165 Post Street, San Francisco, CA 94108.

Index

*B*ill Gleeson is a fourth-generation Californian who grew up traveling the backroads of the Central Valley and the gold country. Gleeson's intimate knowledge of the state's byways and hamlets led to the publication of Small Hotels of California, for Chronicle Books in 1984.

A graduate of California State University, Chico, Gleeson currently resides on the Central Coast, where he works in the field of public relations.

All photographs by the author, except for the following, used by permission: Adler Fels, page 20, courtesy Adler Fels; Husch Vineyards, page 48, courtesy Husch Vineyards; Navarro Vineyards, page 44, courtesy Navarro Vineyards; Sierra Vista Winery, page 142, courtesy Sierra Vista Winery;   Edmeades Winery, page 46, courtesy Edmeades Winery.

Winery drawings by Jean Gier; "How Wine is Made" diagram courtesy Sebastiani Vineyards, Sonoma, California.